Schooling the Estate Kids

STUDIES IN PROFESSIONAL LIFE AND WORK
Volume 7

Editor
Ivor Goodson
Education Research Centre, University of Brighton, UK

Editorial Board
J. M. Pancheco, *University of Minho, Portugal*
David Labaree, *Stanford University*
Sverker Lindblad, *University of Gothenburg*
Leslie Siskin, *NYU/Steinhardt Institute for Education & Social Policy*

Scope
The series will commission books in the broad area of professional life and work. This is a burgeoning area of study now in educational research with more and more books coming out on teachers' lives and work, on nurses' life and work, and on the whole interface between professional knowledge and professional lives.

The focus on life and work has been growing rapidly in the last two decades. There are a number of rationales for this. Firstly, there is a methodological impulse: many new studies are adopting a life history approach. The life history tradition aims to understand the interface between people's life and work and to explore the historical context and the socio-political circumstances in which people's professional life and work is located. The growth in life history studies demands a series of books which allow people to explore this methodological focus within the context of professional settings.

The second rationale for growth in this area is a huge range of restructuring initiatives taking place throughout the world. There is in fact a world movement to restructure education and health. In most forms this takes the introduction of more targets, tests and tables and increasing accountability and performativity regimes. These initiatives have been introduced at governmental level – in most cases without detailed consultation with the teaching and nursing workforces. As a result there is growing evidence of a clash between people's professional life and work missions and the restructuring initiatives which aim to transform these missions. One way of exploring this increasingly acute clash of values is through studies of professional life and work. Hence the European Commission, for instance, have begun to commission quite large studies of professional life and work focussing on teachers and nurses. One of these projects – the Professional Knowledge Network project has studied teachers' and nurses' life and work in seven countries. There will be a range of books coming out from this project and it is intended to commission the main books on nurses and on teachers for this series.

The series will begin with a number of works which aim to define and delineate the field of professional life and work. One of the first books 'Investigating the Teacher's Life and Work' by Ivor Goodson will attempt to bring together the methodological and substantive approaches in one book. This is something of a 'how to do' book in that it looks at how such studies can be undertaken as well as what kind of generic findings might be anticipated.

Future books in the series might expect to look at either the methodological approach of studying professional life and work or provide substantive findings from research projects which aim to investigate professional life and work particularly in education and health settings.

Schooling the Estate Kids

Carl Parsons
University of Greenwich, London, UK

SENSE PUBLISHERS
ROTTERDAM/BOSTON/TAIPEI

A C.I.P. record for this book is available from the Library of Congress.

ISBN: 978-94-6209-011-8 (paperback)
ISBN: 978-94-6209-012-5 (hardback)
ISBN: 978-94-6209-013-2 (e-book)

Published by: Sense Publishers,
P.O. Box 21858,
3001 AW Rotterdam,
The Netherlands
https://www.sensepublishers.com/

Cover design by Holly Zarnecki: http://hollyzarnecki.moonfruit.com/

Printed on acid-free paper

TABLE OF CONTENTS

ACKNOWLEDGEMENTS

This book was researched and written in pursuit of a passion, an affection for an under-rated and overlooked area and its people and a deeply felt anger at enduring, institutional, politically contrived, deceitful injustice. The book owes most to the residents of the Newington and neighbouring estates in Ramsgate, Thanet in north-east Kent, and the professionals associated with the The Conyngham School which became The Ramsgate School and in 2005 The Marlowe Academy. I was made very welcome in the community, in homes, centres, offices and workplaces. I have intruded into people's lives in a way I hope was at all times respectful. The many hours spent in the Marlowe Academy, shadowing students as they went from class to class, interviewing, either by appointment or through chance encounters, was a delight. I am most grateful for the forbearance, generosity and openness of staff and students.

I interviewed many who had worked in the Conyngham or Ramsgate Schools and got their stories which varied across a range of emotions from joy through frustration to survival and even guilt. Past pupils dug into memories which were hugely varied. It added valuably to my notes of visits to the school over ten years and resonated with how I was impressed with survival skills well beyond my own and sadness that things became so bad and were apparently so difficult to alter. Out of all these efforts to tell the story of the estates and the school which was to serve them, I am acutely aware that the duration and depth of my association with the school is small compared with those who have lived and worked in Newington or its secondary school. Many teachers have recognised that the school has been and still is exceptional on many counts and have said that they should have written a book about it. But they did not. And this is probably not the book they would have written.

Many of those I have written about have read through parts of the text and commented, telling me what I had got wrong, omitted or over- or understated. Others have dug out documents for me or processed data and tolerated my requests for more and more. Kent's Information Management Unit was particularly helpful.

In developing the book, four people have read parts or the whole and fed back perceptively and helped me avoid naivety, exaggeration or timidity. I hope I have responded appropriately in crafting the book to avoid these weaknesses. Peter Carver applied his journalistic skills to sections and encouraged me to write for *every*one, not just a narrow academic audience, to 'get quite porky' about conclusions and not to write of 'a digging implement' when I meant, or should have meant, 'a spade'. I might not have understood the phrase properly. David Ewens, a novelist at heart and with a keen eye for equal opportunities language, could spot the subtleties that would not work and the under-statements that would go unnoticed unless beefed up. Most telling was his constant correction when I used rather de-humanising phrases like 'the working class' or 'the poor'. You will see that it is 'working class people' or 'poor people'. These are not just subtle changes but important if respect for all is to be present throughout. Paul Welsh could spot a factual error in relation to the local scene, having a history in the area's education arrangements that goes back decades. He had insights into the unmoving, even unmovable, ills of Thanet as well as into the political forces at work.

My biggest debt is to Stephen Steadman who read every word more than once. He put several weeks' full time equivalent work into just tidying up my words and my thinking and even more in commenting wisely on the shape of the final product and visual presentation. He has been a key influence in my publications over 30 years and it is rare to get that good humour and intelligence always so freely given. I am grateful to him for that.

Finally, I must thank Canterbury Christ Church University and the University of Greenwich for the intellectual environments and the interest and support colleagues.

GLOSSARY

ADHD	Attention Deficit and Hyperactivity Disorder
ASBO	Anti Social Behaviour Order
ASD	Autistic Spectrum Disorder
AST	Advanced Skills Teacher
BTEC	Business and Technical Education Certificate
CAMHS	Child and Adolescent Mental Health Service
CAT	Cognitive Abilities Test
CCTV	Closed Circuit Television
CSE	Certificate of Secondary Education
DCSF	Department for Children, Schools and Families
DfE	Department for Education
EAL	English as an Additional Language
EBD	Emotional and Behavioural Difficulties
EMA	Education Maintenance Allowance
FE	Further Education
FIFA	Federation of International Football Associations
FLO	Family Liaison Officer
FSM	Free School Meals
FSP	Foundation Stage Profile
GCSE	General Certificate of Secondary Education
HMI	Her Majesty's Inspectorate [of Schools]
ICT	Information and Communications Technology
KCC	Kent County Council
KS 3	Key Stage 3 – curriculum and assessment 11–14
KS 4	Key Stage 4 – curriculum and assessment 14–16
LEA	Local Education Authority
LM	Learning Mentor
L/O	Learning Objective
MAAC	Marlowe Assessment and Achievement Centre
NEETs	Not in Education, Employment or Training
NQT	Newly Qualified Teacher
OECD	Organisation for Economic and Cultural Development
OFSTED	Office for Standards in Education
PCSO	Police Community Support Officer
PIP	Parents in Partnership
PSHE	Personal, Social and Health Education
SCC	Schools in Challenging Circumstances
SEBD	Social Emotional and Behavioural Difficulties
SFECC	Schools Facing Extremely Challenging Circumstances
SEF	Self Evaluation Framework
SEN	Special Educational Needs

GLOSSARY

SENCO	Special Educational Needs Coordinator
SMT	Senior Management Team
SOA	Super Output Area
TUPE	Transfer of Undertakings ~ Protection of Employment
TVEI	Technical and Vocational Education Initiative
UNICEF	United Nations International Children's Emergency Fund

PREFACE

Carl Parsons' book is an important contribution to the education debate and fills one of the most salient and significant voids in much of the policy making of the current government. Although he evokes the origins, evolution and location of what was once The Conyngham School, became the Ramsgate School and began again as the Marlowe Academy, he places this historical trajectory in a wider context.

This book is important because it addresses a vortex in the current educational discourse. The callous disregard of poverty is currently being vividly illustrated by the attempt to change child poverty statistics. Parsons' book asks us once again to confront the continuing issue of how poor people are given substandard education. It was to address concerns such as this that welfare states were constructed and educational policies following the post-war settlement sought to provide equality of opportunity for all. In the current conjuncture, inequality is being massively sponsored and the pursuit of decent education for disadvantaged people is falling to the bottom of the ladder of priorities. Parsons' book eloquently shows how, in his words, 'the punitive "driving up standards" policy in England and the refusal to address family poverty as the root of underachievement of poor children' is displacing any systematic attempt to provide decent education for poor people.

Through a painstaking analysis of one school we get a sense of how a particular neighbourhood can be systematically deprived of reasonable educational opportunities. What is most important about the book is the way that Parsons moves beyond this local and particular study to provide a series of more broadly applicable criteria and procedures for pursuing social justice. In his final chapter, he pulls together a set of policy proposals and guidelines which are of enormous import for those who continue to pursue social justice.

Ivor Goodson
Professor of Learning Theory
Education Research Centre
University of Brighton

INTRODUCTION

There are many reasons for writing this book. One motive for taking my pension from my post as Professor of Education at Canterbury Christ Church University was to pursue this particular passion – no one would pay me to do it! The Conyngham/Ramsgate School and the Newington estate in Thanet, Kent saddened me, but I had an affection and respect for both. They battled in circumstances of inequality and neglect which were not of their making.

I grew up on a council estate in the 1950s and 60s. I went to the grammar school 12 miles away, stayed on to the sixth form and went to university, not knowing quite what either of those two steps involved. They were different times but there was still the strangeness for the working-class child joining with, and being relatively successful at, the education game.

At Canterbury Christ Church, still largely a teacher education college in the 1980s, The Conyngham School in Ramsgate was legendary as a really tough assignment for any secondary student teacher on placement. It was no less of a challenge in the 1990s when it became The Ramsgate School, but I had no direct experience of it until 1999 when we had a small project working with French university colleagues comparing provision for children *at risk* in Thanet and Lille. In 1997 and 2003, The Ramsgate School was in the national press as the worst secondary school in England with 1%, then 4% of pupils achieving the government benchmark of 5 A*-C GCSE grades.

My first encounters with The Ramsgate School and the Newington estate left me with profound concerns for these children, the provision that failed them and for the estate that failed to thrive and did not get the investment, support and service it should have had. For two years from 2006, we had a much larger international project which attempted to address some of the needs so evident in this pupil population. It is a sad reflection that, six years later, it would be difficult to detect any impact that our project made, despite what amounted in total to £1 million of resources.

The concerns, the worries, even the guilt, and increasingly the anger stayed with me and were part of the impulse to study and write about what became The Marlowe Academy. The book examines from a historical perspective why a school should fall to such depths and how schools in such deprived circumstances are developed and sustained over time to the detriment of the communities they should serve. This is not inner city but outer urban in a rich county. It is but one example of the estimated 100 plus secondary schools in England, out of nearly 4,000, that face extremely challenging circumstances.

The book is a sociological study but written, I hope, in such a way that anyone concerned with the provision of education in poorer communities might relate to it. The book has three main levels of focus: firstly, the community and the families who should come first in any thinking about the provision of government-funded services designed to meet the needs and further the interests of the populace; secondly, the school and its history, looking at how it started out in 1963 full of hope to serve what was partly a mining community on the edge of a relatively new estate; thirdly, the political environment run by which ever political party and their failure to make the lives of the people living in these communities better able to benefit from what schooling has to offer.

Schooling of the Estate Kids is a title adapted from Pat Thomson's *Schooling the Rustbelt Kids (*2002) which, as Pat herself said, was taken from Paul Corrigan's 1979 title, *Schooling the Smash Street Kids*. All three, mine and these two, are different, yet joined by the fact that sociologists have over all these years enjoyed (I mean that) reporting on the underachievement of the poor in education. Make no mistake, this is a tragedy and a scandal. The existence of such schools leads to diminished life chances of children attending them and these schools are allowed to persist through a collusion of those who want to blame poor people and the vested interest of those higher up the scale in not losing resources to those lower down the scale.

The grammar school system is as divisive now as when the original arguments were put forward for comprehensivisation and the common school. In Thanet, the existence of three grammar schools has been a significant contributor to the gradient of popularity of schools and enabling the quasi-market in Thanet education all the more easily to direct the needier young people to the schools with the most problems. It might be said that those who have attended grammar schools, as I and my children did, have been 'bought off' or had a critical edge dulled, content to wallow in life's advantages that this early selection bestowed.

Figure 1.1 below, sets out a timeline some key events at the level of the school and nationally. It presents in compressed form the history of the Conyngham School which became The Ramsgate School and, in 2005, The Marlowe Academy. Across four defined periods Labour, Conservative or Coalition governments there has been decline and rebirth, improvement and further distress attributable to the disregard and largely misdirected effort of politicians. The Education Reform Act, free competition in education and the publication of league tables contributed to difficulties faced by the school, bringing it to awful depths in the late 90s and early 2000s. Then six years of improvement as an academy was blasted again by unhelpful national targets and a lack of understanding of and sympathy for the largely vocational curriculum designed for the school.

Researching this book has been a delight because of the people that I have encountered at the community centre, the Sure Start centre, the primary schools or the secondary school itself. The families have been a particular joy to work with, revealing as they did their problems, hopes and achievements. The book covers a span of local educational history from 1963 to 2011.

Throughout that period there has been a concern for, first the early leavers, then the under-achievers and latterly the disaffected and the deprivation-related attainment gap. With separate school types until the 1960s there were also separate examinations systems: Certificate of Secondary Education (CSE) and General Certificate of Education (GCE), reinforcing difference with the CSE only coming in

1965 to give some certification to children who would previously have had none –
and did not until the raising of the school leaving age in 1973.

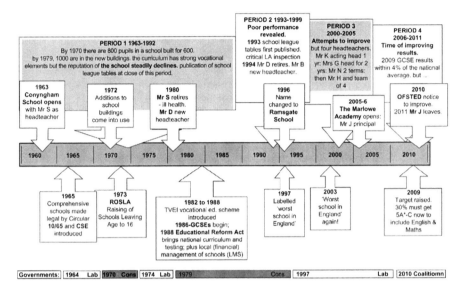

Figure 1.1. Timeline 1963 to 2011 Secondary schooling on Newington Estate, Thanet, Kent.
Three school names; eight headteachers.

The school went through four defined periods. It could be regarded as experiencing
decline after its first decade but for 30 years it functioned adequately enough in
this divided Kent education system while being the least popular school. In a
period of seven years (1992–9), during which time it changed its name from
Conyngham to Ramsgate, it felt the harshness of the publicised league tables at the
same time as there was increasing deprivation in the local estates and increasing
pressures on it as the 'receiving school' – for newcomers, excluded pupils and any
without a school place. It was a period when older staff left and recruitment, never
easy, became a real challenge.

While it had been inspected and found to have 'serious weaknesses' in 1997 it
soon bounced back but in the 2000–5 period the school faced huge difficulties not
least having four headteachers during these six years. This was a bumping along
the bottom and barely surviving period, lifted out in the final year by extreme
measures seldom seen in schools. The Marlowe Academy opened in September
2005 and showed year on year improvements, scuppered by changing targets set
for schools and it, too, found itself with a notice to improve in 2010.

The book looks, in Chapter 2, at the area and the particular issues it faces in
relation to prosperity and educational progress. Chapter 3 focuses mainly of three
families as illustrating their lives, struggles, character and achievements.
Chapters 4, 5 and 6 follow the school's progress through the periods, changes of
headship, changing demands and, mostly, declining fortunes. Chapters 7 and 8

examine the establishment of the Marlowe Academy and how it functioned in an inclusive fashion to give an ever-improving education to the neighbourhood's children. Chapter 9 takes lessons from this one school and sees how they apply to the enduring problems of improving schools in extremely challenging circumstances. Chapter 10 deals with students and parents and what they want and think they get from education while Chapter 11 makes the charge that schools like the Conyngham, Ramsgate and Marlowe are made and sustained by national and local political will. Insufficient resources and resolve nationally are allocated to these areas which suffer from so many social and financial ills.

The postscript adds an account of the 2011/12 school year after the Marlowe's Principal of six years had departed, the results were deemed too poor and Ofsted had given the Academy a 'notice to improve'. In brief, this section looks at the pressures the Academy was under, the changes that were made and the GCSE results that were achieved and published in August 2012.

I hope the book does justice to the time and access that so many people gave me and will persuade others to share the anger and channel it in ways to ensure that children who come from backgrounds which did not best dispose them towards education get the early and continued support to increase their social mobility and improve life chances, whatever the socio-economic status of the family into which they were born.

Reducing child poverty, narrowing the gap and increasing social mobility will not happen with the policies in place in 2012. The UK is a long way from being a fair society, much less fair than most of our European neighbours. An academic might coolly conclude that it should not be so. An ordinary person might be embarrassed by it. A wise citizen should be angered by it.

Schooling the Estate Kids tries both to recognise the local and particular but also to place the school and its neighbourhood in a wider historical and national context. The book's message is that deprived communities do not happen by accident: they are deliberately created and sustained and the schools serving them are under-resourced. Some of the causes lie with the selective disregard of international comparisons, especially with regard to child poverty and social mobility. Together with the ridiculous emphasis on narrow school improvement, they are malign political and intellectual deceits which sustain tragic and unjust outcomes for poorer people.

AN ESTATE OF MIND

WHERE ARE WE?

The Marlowe Academy, which is the focus of this book, is in Thanet, tucked away in the north east corner of Kent, its coast washed by the Thames in the north and the Channel on the East. It is isolated, with its own variety of 'Estuary English'. The local population fondly refers to the place as 'Planet Fannit'.

No one ever stumbled across Thanet as they travelled to another destination. In an atlas, if Kent may be pictured as a roast turkey facing west to Greater London and Surrey, Thanet would be the parson's nose. Nevertheless, the area has some well known landmarks. In the Second World War, fighter pilots reached for the skies from RAF Manston. North Foreland regularly features in the BBC's shipping forecasts. Charles Dickens' Bleak House is on the north side of Broadstairs, in the far north-east of Thanet, where you can also find John Buchan's 39 steps. And there are two other old seaside resorts, Ramsgate and Margate whose faded glory, despite recent efforts at revival notably encouraged by Tracey Emin when the £17M Turner Contemporary Arts Centre opened in 2011, have long since been spurned by fickle holidaymakers lured by more youthful, warmer continental charms.

Thanet has been home to other famous names. The Marchioness Conyngham – whose family name was given to the first school on the site of the Marlowe Academy – was George IV's favourite mistress. She achieved an interesting degree of notoriety.[1] Pugin, architect of the Victorian Gothic Palace of Westminster in the 19th Century, lived in Thanet, and much earlier, St Augustine landed there on a papal mission to bring Christianity to England.

Although the area still hangs onto some light industry, it has lost many of its traditional sources of employment. The shell fish industry has all but disappeared, and the coal mines have all closed, eliminating the 'aristocrats of the working class' as a group, although some households still receive the coal allowance which, when taken as cash, amounts annually to £500, helpful to any ex-miner or their widow. The oil-fired power station at Richborough, has been decommissioned and its cooling towers demolished. From 1988, Pegwell Bay housed the one-time famous Hovercraft port, which closed for lack of business after five years The port of Ramsgate has found it hard to flourish in competition with Folkestone and Dover only 20 kilometres south and the Eurotunnel option has taken away passenger and freight traffic. At the time of writing, the huge Pfizer's pharmaceutical plant, which once employed 7,500 in the Thanet area, is also in the process of closing down.

In the towns of Thanet – Margate, Ramsgate and Broadstairs – the large Victorian houses, once good for the bed and breakfast, bucket and spade holiday makers, now serve small businesses that house children sent out of London's boroughs by social services concerned for the children's welfare. Some areas have large proportions of refugees and asylum seekers. Fostering has been described as the area's current main industry, and Kent CC has recently complained to the London boroughs about overuse of an agreement that Kent would place such children.

One of the few stable industries in the area is the longstanding market gardening and vegetable business. Thanet Earth has recently opened alongside the A253 that brings traffic into Thanet from the west. Its advertising literature describes the largest greenhouse development in the UK with enough glass to cover 80 football pitches. A big hope is that Manston airport, now-a-days occasionally used for charter jumbo jets, will become a Chinese business centre for warehousing, import and export. The Marlowe Academy, and the Newington estate in which it is situated, is not far from there.

Efforts have been made to foster economic regeneration. The A299 has been extended and made dual carriageway at great expense, The high speed train now crosses Thanet en route to Canterbury, and reduces the journey time to London St Pancras to as little as 76 minutes. Business premises have been built – but remain empty. Government grants enabled Canterbury Christ Church University to build a campus to take higher education to the people in 'areas of low participation.' But it is rare to find it bustling with students. Infrastructure is not the problem.

Maybe the problem is a compound of location, and the consequent mindset of the area's population. Thanet is a far out corner with few attractions and indifferent weather. Businesses did not rush to locate there during the boom years from 1997, and the population does not embrace the levels of affluence that would enable them to broaden their horizons. There is a very constrained and inward looking approach to life, with most needs being met within the immediate area. To be able to afford to commute to London or Canterbury a well-paid job is required, and obtaining one of those requires a good standard of education.

THE BUILT ENVIRONMENT

The Newington, Whitehall and Highfields estates cluster together on the outskirts of Ramsgate. In fact, as indicated on the map in Figure 2.1, the estates are rather removed from the three main seaside towns. They consist of 1700 dwellings in total, mostly semis or maisonettes, with one tower block, Staner Court, which is visible from afar but not talked of with much affection. The newest and largest of the three estates is Newington, built mostly in the 1950s. Princess Margaret visited in June 1950 to turn the first sod of the building site, and the boulevard running down the middle for a full mile is the Princess Margaret Avenue. This is a type of boulevard seen in many large out of town estates, with grass down the middle, trees of various sorts, and a generous width to the whole scene. Better that way maybe than tightly packed houses overlooking each other with no space to breathe. But the breadth, the grass and the trees kid no-one. There is a certain pointlessness to it: you can't play on it; you can't park on it.

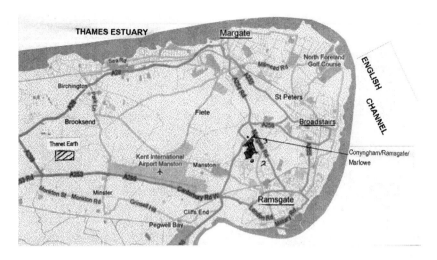

Figure 2.1. Annotated Map of Thanet.

This avenue is broken only by the roundabout where St John's Avenue cuts across what is called 'The Centre', a real address. A local pub closed in 2009. There is a small parade of shops, a mixture of smartness and steel-shuttered permanent closure. The whole is being redeveloped and the flats above the shops were all boarded up in readiness in 2011. Once the estate had all the regular food shops but with a full size Tesco on the southern edge of the estate, they are gone. A Children's Centre, a police sub-station and two large primary schools serve the estates. The former Conyngham Secondary School's functional 1960s building once stood here. It has now been demolished to become a sports area alongside its replacement, the new yellow striped, curved-roofed Marlowe Academy which was built in 2005 and opened for use in September 2006.

Newington is full of solidly constructed, cream-painted 1950s council houses, some with what look like balconies. In the neighbourhood at 8:30 am, children can be seen moving towards their schools, small ones accompanied by parents mostly, and the older children walking towards the Marlowe Academy some stopping in groups, the odd smoker, that collection of young people unsupervised doing young people things. Well maintained houses and gardens predominate with only the occasional overgrown garden and boarded up window. Three bedroom houses here typically sell for £120,000 (2011 prices), and in the whole estate approximately 55% are owner-occupied. The three estates have a population of around 5,000, with a greater proportion of younger people than is average for Thanet as a whole.

The English history of public housing is important and the Newington estate is part of this. Elsewhere in England, there are homes built by benevolent employers. Most striking amongst these are the Quaker estates and the ideology which lay behind their creation. Examples are: Rowntree's New Earswick neighbourhood outside York; Port Sunlight in the Wirral built by the washing powder magnates,

7

the Lever brothers; Bourneville in Birmingham; and the Clark (shoes) Street village in Somerset. Each accompanied the provision of homes, with facilities for education, leisure and a civic hall. The generosity (and temperance) of these morally-based developments seemed less in evidence in the later big estates in London, Birmingham, Newport, Bristol and Park Hill in Sheffield.

The boom era of council house building was post-war, particularly from 1948 onwards. Whilst prefabs were an initial stop-gap for the returning victorious soldiers and the baby booming couples, and though these much loved dwellings served in many areas into the 70s, generously proportioned public housing was built all over the country according to the space and design requirement of the Parker Morris standards from 1961. In that much of the population had lived in rented accommodation before the Second World War, the transformation by the mid 70s was astonishing in its scale and spread, and its impact on social organisation.

It is not too fanciful to compare the English estates with the grand schemes for housing the working poor, or the too poor to buy, elsewhere in the world. The Karl Marx-Hof complex in Vienna and Le Corbusier blocks in Marseille and elsewhere brought art and a certain imaginative generosity to design for collective living. Public housing in Amsterdam, Germany, Italy and Spain has similar impressive historical origins which became over time more functional and industrial after 1945. There was an element of warehousing of people and the withdrawal of state sponsorship of quality housing, though many of the houses for the post war families were much better than the housing they replaced. Two million local authority houses were built in the UK before 1939. After 1945, four million dwellings were built, but that was only sufficient to replace those destroyed in the war. From 1936 to 1961, the proportion of families living in council houses grew from 10% to 26%. They were the houses for working class people. Often they were built on the edge of towns and cities where they would not affect private housing values. The estate was a significant housing environment where rents were a little below market values and the subsidy was in many respects a compensation for, or recognition of, lower incomes. With over one quarter of the population living on council estates little stigma attached to those who lived in them.

Although there were sales of council houses in the early 1970s, the 'right to buy' policy of the 1980s brought reductions in price based on years as a tenant to the extent that 2.2 million were sold between 1979 and 1996. Home ownership of all sorts grew from 10% to 67% during the course of the twentieth century. That has changed the tone and feel of some estates more than others, but many of these neighbourhoods house poor people.

The idea of 'council estate' has always been evocative, whether for past or current residents, house purchasers, school seekers or distant middle classes. Lindsay Hanley describes the ambivalence of people towards the estates where they once lived or relations still live. She mentions a sense of stigma and asserts that 'Council estates are … a physical reminder that we live in a society that divides people up according to how much money they have to spend on shelter'. Of the estate, Hanley says, 'It's a lifelong state of mind' (p. 4) and later refers to a sense of living there as, 'the wall in the head'. For many who came from rented public housing, there is a feeling that that is where you belong – and if you got away it was because of undeserved luck whether through educational achievement, job progression, marriage or inheritance.

The schools which serve estates have their own character and the middle class notions of effort and cleverness are not the reasons for 'working class underachievement'. There is a class-clash. Evans[2] illustrates the construction, staffing, expectations of the school as so distant from the experiences of the estate child and estate family, their economy and best loved activities. We are talking generalities here. The school so often does not serve the children coming into it and grindingly laments the deficiencies the children arrive with and seem unable to shake off. Part of being a professional is shrugging off the taint of the working class, though for many there is a quiet pride in having emerged from it oneself.

The Runnymede Trust report of 2009,[3] provocatively entitled, *Who cares about the white working class?* invites the answer, 'We all do', but can easily lead on to cynical reasons about the desire to avoid crime, teenage pregnancy, ASBOs and all the ills which are seen as welling up from the working class or even workless estates. Even the more 'respectable', waged elements of publicly housed working class people are mildly scorned for their giant plasma TV screens which are always on, the smoking, and the teenagers with horrifically expensive trainers glowing beneath their best track suit bottoms. Then there is the rough talk, the dropped initial consonants, so-called glottal stops and 'innit's'. None of this need reduce their value as human beings, or inhibit respect that professionals and strangers might give them.

There is an amazing amount of detailed Super Output Area (SOA) statistics which focus down to the level of estates. These statistics show that Thanet is the poorest district in Kent and trend data give little indication that things have improved over recent years. When unemployment rises in the region, it rises proportionately more in Newington. It makes an already struggling area struggle more. Four areas in Thanet *always* receive mention as the areas of deprivation and problems. These are Cliftonville West, Dane Valley (Millmead estate), Margate Central and Newington. They come up every time as the lower income, poorer health, lower educational achievement, and higher crime areas. SOA 013B, Newington, has double even the Thanet percentage claiming a benefit, four times the national rate. One estimate for 2011 was that 41% of households were workless and this was expected to rise to 51%. Incapacity benefits are twice the Thanet rate and three times the national rate. The assessed achievement of five year-olds entering school is very low. All the Ofsted reports remark on this. Furthermore, at age 16 their percentage achievement of 5+A*-C grades at GCSE stands at a little over half the national average. This statistic covers whatever school they went to and not just the Marlowe Academy. Teenage pregnancies are higher here and the proportion of these young girls who go on to have their babies is also higher than for other areas in Kent. This address, and these postcodes are associated with measures of potentially life-diminishing deprivation. I could go on.

Against this, one must recognize that the variety of individuals contributing to aggregate statistics is central to an understanding of how a neighbourhood functions. Still it is a minority on unemployment benefit, a quarter still do achieve the national benchmark in school examinations at 16, and most girls do not get pregnant before 18. The average statistics also do not mean that there is no joy or that personal resources are not considerable. To live here, bring up a family, show that togetherness and bond of self-help and to look forward with ambition and optimism for one's children is impressive and invariably evident. The three families described in Chapter 3 illustrate this.

POVERTY IN THE UK

Poverty is not a state of mind but a real, physical experience of limitation. Poverty is a problem and cannot be disguised by calling it social exclusion. Poverty is often, if not exactly an inherited condition, one more likely to be experienced by those whose parents were poor. Poverty affects people's health and, on average in the UK, practically all diseases strike earlier at more people the lower their social class. Heart disease, cancers and mental health problems including depression affect the poorest people most, and those in what used to be called social class five live an average of 12 years less than those in social classes one and two. So poor people live on average more painful and less happy and shorter lives. In terms of learning, achievement at school and the life chances that go with that, it is calculated that by 22 months babies born in the lowest social classes are already measurably behind those in more affluent areas. As you go through the schooling system there is no catch up for most.

Poverty matters from the earliest age and things you do not learn before you are two, you will struggle to learn later. The 'school readiness' of children from poorer families at age 5 is well below that of children from better off homes. There is no catch-up by the end of primary school and attainment at 16 shows the same marked class/income difference, no matter what the aspirations for 'closing the gap' may be. Parental and family circumstances are persistently found to have a heavy impact on attainment in school. In 2002, 77 per cent of children in year 11 in England and Wales (16 year-olds) with parents in higher professional occupations gained five or more A* to C grade GCSEs. This was more than double the proportion for children with parents in routine white collar and manual occupations (32%). In 2009, the gap remained as large as ever with 54% of the 500,000 pupils not eligible for free school meals reaching the 5A*–C including maths and English and only 27% of the 74,000 entitled to free school meals achieving that level. The attainment gap is given as 27.4%. We know too that exclusions from school for discipline reasons also vary by levels of deprivation.

There are many ways in which delinquency, early pregnancy and worklessness haunt some areas of any town. The National Equality Panel (2010) reported that 'the profound gaps in all economic outcomes between more and less disadvantaged areas' imply huge disparities in collective resources. The 'neighbourhood renewal agenda itself needs renewal.'

All four countries of the United Kingdom appear to share in this phenomenon of gross inequality, inequality of wealth and income that is greater than that of almost all other countries in Europe, but exceeded by the United States in this and many other social ills.

The Spirit Level[4] also makes the point that more equal societies do better at almost everything. International evidence shows that in more unequal countries:

– more people suffer from mental illness,
– use of illegal drugs is more common,
– teenage births rates are higher,
– homicides are more common,
– there is more conflict between children,
– more people are imprisoned,
– social mobility is lower, and
– health and social problems are more common.

Life expectancy and infant mortality are also related to inequality. Infant mortality rates are lower in all occupational classes in Sweden than in England and Wales[5] (1992) where they show a consistent rise as you go down the social scale.

As an example, the UK social class differences in women's obesity can be seen all the way up the social ladder: put crudely, the poorer you are the fatter you are. In rich countries, life expectancy is unrelated to spending on health care; it is to do with the place in the hierarchy, the value given to each life and the felt sense of belonging and worth of the individuals.

Poverty excludes. Relative poverty is associated with many negative outcomes for young people. Poverty and inequality stem from a set of cultural and political decisions in which we all in some way collude. High levels of both are conditions which create disaffection, exclusion and resistance. To compound this situation, the UK has an appalling record for demonising the young.

Where parents are poorly prepared by their own experience of parenting to bring up children, where they have challenging circumstances, where they have poor housing, lack of resources, lack of support, diminished expectations, then it is no surprise that their children also struggle as they grow up. Individuals in areas of deprivation confidently making their way, taking responsibility for their lot and achieving against the odds is exceptional. Intervening with young people to instil personal attributes of resilience or high aspirations is a weak response, aimed too much at fixing individuals, removed too far downstream from the causal challenged economic and social circumstances a society has imposed on estate children's early development.

The corresponding position of professionals working in these areas, where we have created a class of under-privileged, under-achieving and sometimes problematic children and families, is a kind of distancing and lamentation. Multi-agency committees meet regularly to commission services and receive feedback from each other yet, between one meeting and the next, one often wonders which children or families have benefited. The most disturbing aspect of this is the lack of respect which is often shown in the language of professionals when talking about the 'under-class'. This is not universal. I have been heartened to meet a primary school head teacher who said, 'I admire the mothers who live on this estate', with no compromise or conditionality. And I was present when in a Sure Start base one of the workers who came into the office saying, 'Those bloody families,' was told firmly, 'We do not speak about our local people like that.' Such incidents give hope. But there is a sense in which there is the same war on the poor in the UK that Herbert Gans[6] wrote about in 1982 in relation to the United States. There are many reasons given for why we need 'the poor' and benefit from poor neighbourhoods, not least in the provision of jobs for the middle classes to work with the poor people.

In the end, we have to find a new language which reflects a respectful understanding of the condition of all people and is supportive of them in their circumstances. It also requires a huge shift in funding as again, compared with other affluent countries of Europe, our 'social transfers' are far less generous than those of our neighbours. Just as we do not want to pay more than a minimum to 'scroungers', nor do we want to give 'goodies' to 'baddies' when it comes down to poorly behaved children.

We believe that families should be responsible for their children and will be to blame for neglect and abuse. But, more in England than in most other countries, we intervene reluctantly, too late and rarely in a befriending way. The Sure Start effect in itself is probably too mild and partial to prevent the falling behind of babies and very young children. We intervene punitively, severely and late, rather than supportively, educationally and early.[7]

So, how should one pull together the international comparisons, national level information and local experience. Although it is a shocking realisation, it is evident that the UK condones its levels of poverty. Indeed, it creates and sustains them. The cultural mindset of the neo liberal believes we achieve by our own efforts, that we should keep what we earn and somehow those who have little actually deserve little. The belief is that those in high level jobs deserve bonuses: jobless people deserve the threat of a removal of benefits. Countries with more helpful social welfare systems are less judgemental, accept that good fortune and not necessarily deservingness have given most citizens what they have, and have educated their electorates to be more caring of society's lower paid and poorer people. The UK should take a leaf out of their book.

I LIVE ON THE NEWINGTON ESTATE

A COMMUNITY

Many are rightly proud to live on the Newington estate and are aggrieved at its reputation, which many see as undeserved. There is, however, widespread talk around Thanet of the Newington estate being a hotbed of drugs, crime and violence, but it is not the dominating experience of people living there. As one resident put it, 'A chap down the end of our road was put in prison for selling drugs. If I hadn't read it in the paper I wouldn't have known.' It is largely a quiet place where families keep themselves to themselves. An important point to be made is that the experiences of families living in one area will vary massively even if low income is a common factor. Newington has the poorer reputation, partly through being the largest of the three Ramsgate estates, and the one with the shopping area, the gathering point for young people off and on over the years. The houses are slightly cheaper and the car number plates may indicate older vehicles. Still, there are people who settled in Newington, brought up their children, bought their houses and stayed – with still no plans to move away. Even some of these admit to not owning up to the name of the estate when giving their address and postcode. The Newington Residents Association and local councillors are said to have 'clout' and are able to 'make things happen'.

Driving or walking around the spacious Newington estate on a fine day is a pleasant enough experience. Apart from the going to school periods and home time the streets are quiet. In the summer evenings, there is not a lot of hanging around of young people. With the pub gone and many of the shops boarded up around The Centre, there is no obvious gathering point and those inhabitants you see have things to do, places to go or dogs to walk. On a cold winter's night it is bleak and deserted, but no more than other residential areas.

Living on the estate can be hard. It calls on all the resources of individuals and on the collective support that family members can give each other. In all, I had contact with over 20 families, but no family is typical and the three which I describe below offer different perspectives on life in relative poverty, or if one were to put it differently, in diminished financial circumstances. Many would deny labels for the neighbourhood of 'difficult', 'troubled' or 'deprived', and would certainly reject terms applied to individuals or families like 'poor', 'dysfunctional' and 'having no aspirations' as insulting and misunderstanding the estate and its people. As one woman resident put it, 'the people on this estate have hearts of gold'.

In contrast, the media stories were of the ASBO (Anti Social Behaviour Orders) five and how 'this gang was making life miserable for residents on the Newington estate' (BBC News Channel, 26 Aug. 2009). The Thanet Community Safety

Partnership had spent a year gathering evidence from CCTV footage and witnesses. When it came before the magistrate, the orders forbade the five to stand on the pavement outside or to enter the Spar shop in The Centre in Newington. It was the highest number of ASBOs to have been applied at the same time in Kent. It is easy to see how a reputation can be sustained when these situations arise, when the press feeds on them, and when local television arrives to be nearly run out of the estate by angry young people riding their bikes in an intimidating fashion at the cameras and the interviewer.

Then there was the murder outside the Flowing Bowl pub (nicknamed the thrown bottle) in 2007, but people agreed that it was an inter-families thing. 'It's not that if you were an ordinary person walking up there you would get stabbed.' Even so, blogging on the web and the reports of the court case over time keep such incidents in people's consciousness.

The families are described below with particular attention paid to a) the family and relationships including health and contentment b) the neighbourhood c) money d) schooling.

THREE FAMILIES: PAT'S, MILLIE'S AND GINA'S

Pat's family is one that could be regarded as steady and secure. Income is not high but has been regular through the years, and it increased when Pat began her work in a school support role. It is a stable two parent, two children family. Millie's family has lived nearly as long as Pat's on the estate, but their income is low and less secure. She has six children and her partner, long gone and now dead, was never a support. But her children are doing well. Gina's family is large with her five children producing 20 grandchildren only one of whom has reached school leaving age. Trauma, death, depression and trouble with school has always been present. Gina is the core of the family, ever-present to support and advise. They survive and, individually and collectively, can be quite jaunty about life.

Pat's Family – Getting by and Coming Through with no Complaints

Pat has lived on the Newington estate for over 30 years. She and her husband work, as do her children. They own their own home, the one they moved into as tenants when she had small babies.

The family structure is simple as set out below and there are many others on the estate that Pat could point to that are little different. She and her husband Pete are both local, though some would question 'local' with Pete coming from 15 miles along the coast. Their brothers and sisters are mostly local and all are in contact. As Pat put it, 'We are a very functional family right through'. They see each other on and off and send birthday cards to each others' children. They meet up for family events but otherwise get on with their own lives.

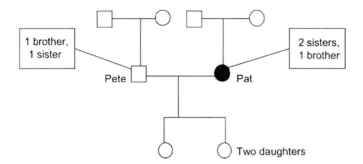

Figure 3.1. Pat's family structure.

Pat's children went to the local primary and progressed through to the Conynham School. They went to clubs and dancing at the community centre. St Christopher's church used to run children's activities in the holiday. Newington Free Church still has a mother and toddlers group.

As for the estate, Pat quickly found that the reality did not match its reputation.

> It had a reputation when we moved in and I can remember, 'Oh, no. I really, really did not want to go there'. My husband said if we did not take that house we would not get a house. We had got to go. The morning we moved in, the neighbours came out and made us tea. The milkman stopped to see if we wanted milk. The people were really friendly and welcoming. I wanted my daughter to carry on at playschool and there was a group at the newly opened community centre. I walked through the door not knowing anyone at all and the people were really, really friendly. I never saw anything really that made me think, Oh, that is why this estate has got the reputation it has. It [the trouble] is in little pockets, I think, mostly around The Centre.

> I felt quite happy to walk up through the estate in the evenings and I didn't feel threatened or concerned. It is a bit of a maze. Children used to gather, up to about five years ago, round The Centre. Quite a few undesirables. There was a shop selling alcohol and the pub across the road. And the chippy; the chap in there only had to go out and have a word and they dispersed. There have been little flare-ups with the kids, but it's never been a no-go area like you see on the television.

In common with many areas, local services have disappeared and there is a greater centralisation of retail which is matched by people's ability and willingness to travel to buy.

> The facilities have gone. When I first moved there, there was a rent office, the doctors' surgery, a chemist, a greengrocer's store, hairdressers, butchers. I used them all the time. I have never driven. I walked there. We've still got the butchers and the general store. The majority of the shops had already gone before Tescos was built at the top end. Oooh, the Pub. I only went in there twice.

A lot of people have bought their own houses (55%) and for many, their children are grown up. It improved the estate, but even so Pat agreed that it was a needy estate.

> I would say there would be quite a lot of needy people on the estate. There are a lot of people who are unemployed. There are a lot of children who have a lot of 'uncles'. There is quite a lot of help going in, though. The help they got from The Ramsgate School when I was there as a teaching assistant and the help they get from the school I am at now, yes, it is quite a lot.

In terms of environmental contentment, Pat had seen improvements.

> I know one thing that has really improved and that is dog mess. … That has improved 100%. There was a rubbish amnesty a while back. There is still a place at the bottom of Stirling Way where you can drop off rubbish and it gets cleared, a sort of informal arrangement.

In terms of crime and drugs, Pat felt that the area was not too bad. She shrugged off any suggestion that it was or ever had been a big problem. The police had a different view but it related to just one or two properties.

Money has never been plentiful. With both incomes it adds up to around £36,000 (2011) and they have to be careful, but less so now. Pete has been in the same skilled manual job for 30 years, on the whole contentedly. Pat worked as an upholstery machinist, then part time in schools, 'I always fitted the working around the children'. They always took family holidays which were mainly camping in the New Forest or south Wales. Now, with the children standing on their own feet, they go further afield and have regular foreign holidays and, if they do go to the old haunts in England, it is to B & B or hotels.

Both her children attended The Ramsgate School. The youngest left in 1990. The school began to 'crack up' after that, she felt.

> They got a really rounded education with good discipline. In the fourth year, they were able to go out to college and do vocational subjects. Both of my children gained qualifications including one with a degree managed through day release from her employer. Both of them still live in the area.

This was a 'reading household' always with books in the house. Earlier they came from the library, but less so as books became more affordable. It is evident that Pat was quite able to help her children with their school work, 'especially at the younger stage – listening to reading, spellings and later with homework. She also provided them with all they needed for lessons, PE kit, pencils, rulers and all that'. Pat's daughters achieved enough at school to get them on a vocational path and both, now in their 30s, are career girls – but might not accept being so labelled. Even when redundancy loomed, they were able to move on to other employment. Both are married.

For Pat, the estate is home and is likely to remain so. She exudes a sense of belonging and contentment that goes back a long way. There is a relaxed, almost peaceful, sense of endearment towards the estate which is where the children were at school, where Pat has always worked and where her husband has nearby employment. This is not a limited life and this is home. There is a very considerable 'localness' about the family, rooted in their domestic haven, not enticed to other regions by ambition, curiosity or 'greener grass', happy with what they know.

Millie's Family – Head Down, Battle on

Millie and her family have lived in their house for 24 years as tenants. It has reportedly always been quiet in this cul-de-sac off the main Princess Margaret Avenue. She has lived in Ramsgate all her life, grew up on the neighbouring estate and went to the Conyngham School. Millie and her partner had six children and the second daughter and her partner have one son. Millie was adopted into a family when very young along with four of her siblings, and considers that she had a secure upbringing. It made a total of eight children. Millie is close enough to some of her sisters to go on holiday with them most years for a week – usually nothing extravagant. There are two sisters and a brother she sees nothing of. Millie had ambitions once. She had wanted to join the army but had never really got back to any sort of training, 'I met their dad first'.

Millie's partner, Mike, died some years ago after a long period of ill-health. He had moved from the family home several years before but remained local. Millie has always been the provider and had little support from her partner/ex-partner, though they remained on reasonable terms, 'Well, you have to for the children's sake'. The family relationships had been amiable enough for one or other of the children in a domestic argument to say, 'Right, I'm off round the corner to dad's!'

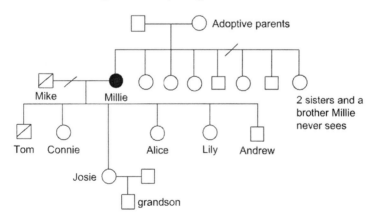

Figure 3.2. Millie's family structure.

On top of the death of the father, a tragic accident killed the oldest son in his early 20s. So the family has had, and dealt with, its moments of great sadness. The children have now all left school. All spent some or all of their secondary schooling at The Ramsgate School or Marlowe Academy and occupied themselves in the local area. All live locally except when away at university but even then the university of choice was one of the local ones for two of the three children who progressed to higher education. Once they were teenagers Millie said, 'The kids did their own thing, once they were old enough'. It seems Millie does not go far – except those holidays – and the children, by and large, 'They don't go to Canterbury or further afield. They just stay local.

> It is nice and quiet in this road, about the quietest place on the estate. Neighbours are fine. Most of them keep themselves to themselves. We always stop to say 'hello' and 'lovely day'. I love it here. We don't do the in and out of each others' houses thing.

Millie talked about looking after her grandchild and was clearly a resource in this respect. 'I look after him any time because I work nights. My daughter lives just round the corner. She has asked if I can look after him on Saturday; I haven't told her yet.'

But of course she will. The sitting room is full of toys for the baby and clearly this grandmothering role is a key part of Millie's life. Connie, as the oldest daughter, 30, was a vocal ally in the parenting. 'I am so proud of my sisters and brother. I tell them so. I do pressure them. I know I am just an older sister.' The three younger ones have been to New York but not their mother. She would love to go. There have been ski trips as well, and when the children come home saying there is this or that happening and has mum got the money, she just says, 'Oh well, more overtime'.

It is a very private, self-sufficient family and Millie is not involved in any groups – 'I don't have the time'. Neither as a child, nor now, had she had any involvement with official services. She says she has never had need of employment offices or the dole or social workers or PCSOs.

Talking about the reputation of estate, Millie said:

> I think it is a lot better than it was. At The Centre, you'd get all the yobs gathering, congregating outside the shops and in the flats you got drug dealers and all that. They've all moved out because they are pulling them down. It's a lot quieter than it used to be. Well I think it is.

Connie had views on the estate

> Me and my friends used to wander down the town and hang around under the flats. They should have used it [the space for car parking] for something but nobody ever did. Around The Centre it was always just a place for hanging around smoking and drinking, but I never had any trouble. I mean, my brother was one of them. I think it was kids with nothing to do and nowhere to go. No one's given them any dreams or ambitions. I just think it's an estate, just an estate. But I think it's all right. We've lived here all the time and mum's brought us up all right. I think it's OK.

She described how community wardens and PCSOs would go around and talk to the kids but acknowledged how hard it was for them. 'They try to talk to the kids, try to be on their level, give it all the chat and all that but the kids must think "whatever", cos they really don't know what they are going through. They have never been in that situation themselves'. Connie found you could make things better if someone went round and asked people what they wanted for their children. There had been some activities at the church over the summer but only for two weeks, 'If that had been on all the time, that would have been great'.

The high points for Millie are the holidays with three of her sisters, just once abroad, and Connie sometimes goes along, raised to the status of fellow sister and enjoying hearing her mum and sisters as they reminisce. These are the 'girls' holidays'. Otherwise Millie does not go to Canterbury or anywhere.

Millie's income amounts to £240 per week which is £158 for 30 hours plus working tax credits. The two children who most recently left the Marlowe sixth form and one working daughter, Connie, live with her.

> It is not a lot to go round. I would not go elsewhere for the money, banks or loan sharks. I suppose I could, but I wouldn't. My view is if you haven't got it, you haven't got it. I budget – this bit goes here and this bit goes there. That's what I do. I stretch it out. It's got to last. I got that from my mother; she'd rob Peter to pay Paul, but Peter got paid as well. If you used something from the cupboard, you replaced it. You never let it run down. If you used a tin of beans, when you went down the shop and you replaced it.

Millie remembers being at The Conyngham School. She recognised 'the snobby part and the common part' – she saw herself as belonging to the latter. Millie recalls the Conyngham School being fine for herself in that less competitive educational environment twenty years earlier, of the 60s and early 70s, though that seems to translate into benign irrelevance. It was as though school did not put her under pressure, did not expect too much and did not deliver much that would count as credits in the jobs market.

> Connie had enjoyed her time at the Conyngham in the early 90s.

> I had a really positive time there. I was friends with everybody from the geeks to the popular people, people I still see today. There's some I see now, even a friend I was at primary school with. The kids who caused the problems – it was just a small number – I could give the names as well. It was just a few of them who spoiled it for the rest of us, tarred us with the same brush. I just think it was that the teachers did not know how to handle them. Well, it wasn't 'handle them' but when you are a teacher you just have to take it. They get sent out of the classroom or they don't come in. They are just lippy to the teachers and they just have to take it. It tarred us with that brush that the school was that bad but it wasn't that bad at all. It wasn't.

She thought the deputy and head were sound, even if some felt the deputy frightening, 'Scary, but he was just strict like teachers should be so people did not mess him around because he said how it was going to be. He was straight down the line. There were no second chances. It was good. I think they should be like that. I never got into trouble so it was all right for me.' Connie recalls a number of the teachers at the Conyngham at that time as 'amazing'. She never remembered being pressured at school, 'not pressured about exams like they are now.' However, they did not have school discos because the boys would play up. 'We had none of the extras.'

Tom, Millie's eldest, 'just wasn't a school person'. Millie described how he would just go into school in the 1990s, get his registration mark and then slip out. The deputy brought him home one day – we are talking about 1993 – and said, 'He's not going to learn. He comes in he gets his mark and he disappears'. There were only three weeks of term left and he said it was not worth him coming in. Tom got a job the next day and stuck to it and is still in it. 'I'm quite proud of him in that way really'.

Josie hardly went for the last year because she suffered with headaches and was 'under the specialist.' She's over that now. She did not like school anyway. Alice, the first to go to university, enjoyed the Marlowe and the younger Lily loves it and 'she tells me everything'. Millie said, rightly proud. 'When I go to open day, they say, "Well there's not much I can tell you. They are fabulous kids and they are doing really well" and I say, "You're not talking about my kids are you?"' She has felt that the school has kept her informed and she has the Principal's mobile number, like all parents. 'It's upstairs somewhere'. Only once did she receive a letter from the school about a 'little problem'. She went in and was treated really pleasantly and the problem was resolved.

Millie and her family will have been amongst the biggest beneficiaries from The Marlowe – the three youngest children all made it to university out of the 100+ from The Marlowe's 6th form: Alice, Lily and Andy.

Alice finished university in 2011, after having taken a year out. Only two of the six in her Alice's group who went to university from The Marlowe made it through to the end. The other was a boy who went to a northern university but came down to finish at Canterbury.

During Alice's time at university, Millie sent money to her, when Alice let it be known she had no money for food. Students at her university could not get jobs because the lectures were 'all over the place'. So Millie was supporting Alice, even if she was sometimes on the edge. Though Alice had received her £1,000 up front, the bursary from the Marlowe sponsor Roger de Haan, it did not last long. There was 'freshers week' and, as she said, 'I couldn't just stay at home'. Then there were other events and the summer ball with all the dressing up and expense that went with that. And mum helped out.

After his law degree, Andy, the youngest son, had the ambition to get a job and earn some money, but had not identified a target for where he would want to live and work. Then again, he wondered if he would continue with the degree at all.

Connie is doing what she always wanted to do, working with young children. From school, she went to college but dropped out when her brother was killed in an accident 'grieving and all that'.

Then I thought, 'I need money'. I wanted to help my mum out, if I'm honest. I'm a helper. Can't help it, soft like my mother. I got a job in a factory and stuck it for three years – I hated it. Then I saw the job in the paper, ... asked my mum to apply for it for me. I was so ... I had no confidence.

When she went to college on the childcare course she knew that was what she wanted to do. She reflected on the fact that she had 'looked after our kids', and from being a Team Support Worker in a special school, she is now a senior. People have encouraged her to become a teacher, but she was put off by 'all that paper work'. After ten years in the job and having moved up a grade, her earnings reached £14,000 (2011).

Connie had a revealing rant about decisions young people on the estate made:

I think this country's a bit mad because everyone who tries to do something, pay their way, they never get any help. I could not afford to live by myself, pay a mortgage but you get these teenage girls who pop babies out and get a house given to them and get their rent paid and all that. It's just wrong. It does not give kids any ambition to do things. You have to strive and strive and people who don't try get it handed to them on a plate. I'm not sure how happy some of them are but some certainly are. That's their dream met, done. But if you want more, you don't seem to get helped, do you know what I mean? It just winds me up, when you see these kids with kids. That winds me up for a start, kids with kids. They should not be having babies. They've lost their life, lost their youth. That's up to them, that's their life but the government allows that to happen.

The resentment here is from close to the scene and, whilst referring to a minority of young people on the estate, is part of Connie's daily experience. While not an analytical response which asks why, or why here, it represents a current of opinion not confined to the national and local press. It also exists within poor communities.

Millie and her family have had to struggle financially, that is clear. That is the standard position and regarded in an uncomplaining way as the likely future. Millie's aspirations for her children are set out simply. 'I'm a cleaner and I worked in the fields, in a taxi office and I wanted them to have something better.' The three youngest in particular are buoyant and hope to 'get on' but, just as importantly, convey the sense that they have been equipped to 'get on'. This does not include any stated intention to get away from Thanet. London does not call. There appears to be an expectation in the family that the good jobs will be available within travelling distance, even though reality says that might not be so.

There was no complaining about the education provision at any stage, not when Millie was a secondary age pupil in the 60s/70s, not at the time of the upheavals when the school was in special measures, and, most notably, not since 2005 when the Marlowe Academy was established. Part of this is an acceptance of what you get and making the best of things. There were no comparisons with other schools or criticisms of their low examination results in the late 90s and early 2000s.

Gina's Family – Struggling On

Gina is very much the hub, the reliable core of her large extended, growing family. Most of her children, aged 26 to 38, live on the estate nearby and it means the daughters and grandchildren often visit.

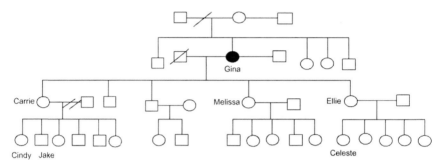

Figure 3.3. Gina's family structure.

Her early life experiences had so many components which are destructive and diminishing. As a woman now in her 50s, she recalled her childhood in a large family with an unreliable mother and an aggressive father. Her mother fled the family home dragging her children after her, but having more interest in her man friends – 'we called them uncle' – than in seeing to her children. Gina showed signs of anxiety and what we would now call anorexia at an early age. Some of her siblings were taken into care and she herself left home at 16. She lost touch with many of her brothers and sisters but has since found a brother. Gina had spent little time in school. She worked in various retail jobs, living in her own bedsit accommodation, and supporting herself. She worked in a chemists for a while but various chemicals caused eczema, the fortunate upshot of which was that she actually went into a tailor's and gained various skills as a seamstress which have stayed with her to the present day. She still has a good quality sewing machine on hand.

She moved to another town with a friend, found work and also found romance and her future husband. She had always been a country and western fan and playing her radio loudly drew the attention of the roofer working on a house opposite. He called out to her to turn the radio up and sang along to some of her favourite songs. Gina was pregnant at 18 and married at 19 and moved to Thanet in 1978. By this time she had two children and three more were to follow. All the children went to primary schools on the Newington estate and all had at least some of their education at the Conyngham School, two of them finishing at the renamed Ramsgate School. The marriage lasted and Gina had various jobs cleaning and working in care homes or hospitals. Her husband remained in work for most of the time and they managed to overcome or ride out most of their difficulties.

In the second decade of the 21st century, Gina was in the same house she had occupied since soon after arriving in Thanet. Her husband died in 2006, collapsing on the pavement in front of a parade of shops. He was 53 and by this time he was working only part-time and having to cope with failing health. Gina's memories of friends are mainly of deaths; so many of her friends have passed away at an early age and in some respects her husband's premature death just seems part of a story of too much poor health, too much cancer, too much not looking after yourself and an early end. Gina feels that she now has no friends outside the house. 'This is my life, this house'. Gina is buying the house, having been a long term council tenant, and her husband's small redundancy payment was sufficient for the deposit.

The family members across three generations support each other and there is the sense of loyalty, even pride. 'My five children are all by the same husband, and there aren't many on this estate who can say that'. Gina's children all live within five miles and three actually live on the estate. Carrie (37), Gina's oldest daughter, moved from a Margate estate to Newington to be closer to her mother and other family members. In all, the five children have a total of 18 children themselves, with ages ranging from newly-born to 16. Gina's house has something of the feeling of a hub about it. As well as her partner and the dog, two of Carrie's six children live with her. Gina says she is always in, as one or more of her grandchildren will always be needing something.

When Carrie came back after special school she got 'a job in the fields' – 'not a proper job.' But then found she was six months pregnant. She has not had a proper job since, and claimed that her keyboarding skills were good when she left the special school, 'but the machines have all changed now.'

Gina talked about the best times, going to the beach, holidays in Malta (Jake had been). They do not travel far but enjoy walking the dogs locally. And Gina is still a big country and western fan.

Talking of the most worrying things, Gina says it is the education of her grandchildren. Jake poses his difficulties: he was on a reduced timetable in Year 9 because of disruption. As she says, when a pupil presents difficulties, the teacher can throw them out. 'Teachers can just get away with it'. Some lessons Jake likes and does well at, including English and maths. He expressed the hope that he would get exam passes in these and others.

Cindy, 16, wanted to get into catering and talked about the food technology teacher who came into school to give them extra tuition. She appreciated that, but felt more teachers could be more understanding, supportive and more giving of their time. She was keen to go to Sheppey College, miles away, where she was convinced she would get the best course according to information from family members. She did not meet the requirements to go into the 6th form at the Marlowe nor sufficient to do her favoured course at any of the further education colleges.

At the start of the Autumn, 2010, things looked a little empty for Cindy, but she and her friends, possibly unrealistic about the options, were not downhearted. There was a sort of restrained resentment that not enough had been done to help them obtain the qualifications required, and then too little help to direct them to opportunities for the future. Now, anything would be a bonus. 'I'll do any job. I'd take any course – engineering, office skills, childcare – but I don't suppose it's available for me'.

Carrie talked about her exclusion from Conyngham after she had put up with three years of bullying. Complaints were made to the head and to 'that deputy, Mr B'. She was punched and kicked and finally 'snapped'; she turned round and stabbed the boy in the arm with a compass and ripped his arm open. Reflecting on the incident, obviously the culmination of much challenge and strife in the school, she felt she had been excluded for 'standing up for myself because of all the bullying. I got punished and they got away with it'. With hindsight, Carrie says, 'I can see the mistake I made, but what was I supposed to do when no one was listening to the cries I was making?'

When excluded, she went to several schools but could not settle and for the last two years of her secondary schooling was at a special residential school 'which was great', where she learnt a lot and, 20 years later, could even reel off the exam passes she got.

Carrie's problems were evident before her exclusion from school and they continued into her later teenage years. The father of her first child was not someone she wanted to have a lasting relationship with; the pregnancy came about through 'a bit of mucking about after the youth club which involved drink and having a laugh', and so Cindy was born and absorbed into the family. Carrie got pregnant again at 18 and moved in for a while with her partner's mother but shortly after the baby was born, the relationship became fractious and Carrie moved back in with mum. Carrie started work briefly while Gina looked after the two children. Things looked promising and, in the end Carrie's social life also looked up, even if it did mean some conflict with her mum and dad and tension over who was to look after the two children.

Life was hard in the family with four children, two grandchildren and two adults on relatively low wages. Sticking together and being supportive was central to the family's principles but presented numerous and unanticipated difficulties. It only needed one of the adults or older children to get sick and it was a struggle to organise who would look after the babies. If Gina and her husband and the older children wanted to go out – and Carrie wanted to as well – then there were 'ructions'. Carrie lost her job, 'Well, it lost me in the end. I couldn't get on with the people there'. And she embarked on a new relationship.

Being older, the hope was that she would settle down, look after her children, be supported by a partner in work, and achieve a stability she had not previously known. But she had two miscarriages in a row and, by the time she conceived again, the latest relationship had become unpleasantly violent, and there were fears for the safety of the children. Carrie was actually put in hospital after one particularly nasty conflict and both social services and police were involved. Carrie is quite defensive in her account of the period, accepting she was as much to blame as her partner, both being still in their early 20s. But there was a third child and a council house was found on another estate into which Carrie moved, with frequent visits from social services. Carrie felt quite lonely out there, two miles removed from the rest of her family.

A fourth child was on the way and, by this time, drink was involved on a regular basis so that the social services people had fears that the older children and the new baby would not be properly cared for. At 24 years old with four children, no earned income, a possessive, unreliable and violent irregular partner, all the ingredients for unhappiness and even despair were present. When Carrie's partner went to prison this provided the break that Carrie needed. But there was something of a void in her life, and she remained without work partly because of the children that she struggled to look after. She was also grappling with alcohol abuse and some mental health problems, being a regular visitor to the GP for tranquillisers and sometimes counselling.

All the while Gina was a constant support in the background, and quite often in the foreground too, especially after Carrie was able to move back to Newington to be nearer her family. Another partner moved in. Another pregnancy and miscarriage were followed by another pregnancy, which went through to a successful birth, and led to both joys and heightened tensions in the household. Big debts were run up and five years later Carrie was still unable to get a credit card because of the bad credit rating of her last partner.

There are now six children. Two live with Cindy, one with another relative, one has been adopted, and two are fostered. While the family as a whole was not happy with the involvement of social services, 'I've had a lot of trouble with those', said Cindy, there have been some emergency steps taken to remove all the children for what was judged to be their own safety. In 2011, Carrie lived round the corner with another new partner and was fairly buoyant about the future. Though resentful of some aspects of her past, she had come to terms with her children being relocated. She sees a lot of her oldest two who live with Cindy, and if there is trouble at school it could be Gina, Carrie or Ellie who go up to the school to 'sort it out'.

Ellie, the youngest of Gina's five children, left school before her GCSEs, The Ramsgate school never having grabbed her. She worked packing fruit and vegetables until she discovered, still 16, that she was pregnant. Bronchial problems and the pregnancy put paid to employment and she went on to have five daughters, 'all by the same dad'. She had asked to be sterilised after number three but, at 23, was told she was too young.

Since moving to slightly more spacious accommodation on the estate, things are a little easier for the six of them. Her partner, who lives separately with his two children by a previous marriage, sees the children frequently and has one each weekend staying with him. He pays for the children's school uniform and shoes. Ellie is happy enough with the housing arrangement living in the 'girl house' and 'I've got used to being able to see what I like on the tele'. The oldest daughter is Celeste, aged 10, who has faced (and posed) the biggest problems for Ellie who does not feel she had the support from the school she should have had. Celeste was often sent home from school for one or several days exclusion and was labelled as ADHD with dyslexia.

Ellie had some support from the Parents in Partnership (PIP) team but that did not work out; they just suggested things that did not work with Celeste. Most helpful was the school Family Link Officer (FLO). 'She's been where I've been', and was not like the others who just kept on saying, 'It's not good enough'. Celeste did not want to go to school and would rub marmite over her uniform so that she would not have to go. The FLO simply said to bring her in her pyjamas so that Ellie would not get into trouble. Beyond the FLO, Ellie could only point to the family as a source of support.

In Ellie's view, the school had not been helpful in getting Celeste statemented. The process only began after she had been permanently excluded. She cannot be medicated until all assessments are done but is happy with her home tutoring; spread over four days it amounts to five hours a week, 'which has worked out a lot better and she has learned a lot'.

Two of Ellie's younger children are a bit behind with their reading, 'But there are learning difficulties in the family on both sides'. The school says they give extra help with reading, 'But they don't'.

Viewing her situation supported by what averages £425 a week, Ellie said, 'I'm happy. I'm fine', and set out her medium term intention:

Once the youngest is in reception, I am going out and I'll get a job, any job. As long as my children see me grafting I don't mind. I'll scrub toilets. I don't mind. My family are workers.

The estate for Ellie has been fine and its bad reputation much exaggerated. When she lived at The Centre, where the young people congregated, if they were noisy, she could look out from her balcony and tell them her kids were asleep and could they keep it down. They would say, 'OK, Ellie', and move on. 'You just have to know how to talk to the children'.

FAMILY LIFE ON THE ESTATE

The account of these three families is enough to show the variety of structures and experiences. Money is tight for them all. The demands made by larger families are immense and the most notable source of support comes from the family members. There is evidence of the hard working stable family earning and paying and supporting children through all the expenses of school and even university. There is evidence of huge challenges with numbers of children and the difficulties that some present which make one wonder at the resilience of parents and grandparents. Where professional support might have been helpful it is notable that very little of it is available or called on and is sometimes felt to be judgemental or inappropriate. Underlying the attitude to professional help, one detects a mix of positions: it is not for us, we should not need it, we should stand on our own two feet. Then there is plain pride and the family.

The families have resources, personal and collective strengths. They are short of money and security that the funds will be there week after week and there are worries that any crises may tip them into debt. There are some instances of not joining with agencies that might have been helpful, Sure Start Children's Centre for example, because others there would then know your business. Overall, poverty is a condition which is *made* and sustained. It affects children's development and educational progress hugely. This is well known. The causal links are not that complex and the case is strong that poor families are not supported sufficiently – even where they do not complain. This is injustice.

THE ECOLOGY OF A SCHOOL IN CHALLENGING CIRCUMSTANCES

AN ESTATE SCHOOL

Areas have their own special evolved character formed by the people who live there and the resources at their disposal, including income and housing. A school drawing in children from the locality will inevitably have much in common with that area, its 'educational culture' and the general levels of affluence and previous educational experience of the people. Experience in the Conyngham School, morphing into The Ramsgate School and transforming into the Marlowe Academy, has been the outcome of the varying levels of tension and acceptance between the professionals of the school, the parents and the children of the estates around the school. The starting positions for the relationship have included levels of poverty and family stability, the changing expectations laid on the schools nationally and the levels of resourcing over the years.

At the same time, there are wider local conditions which prevail and intrusions from national policy which had a much greater impact in the 1990s. In terms of the local provision of secondary schooling across the towns of Margate, Broadstairs and Ramsgate in the 1970s and 80s, there were three layers:

1. three grammar schools, two single sex and one mixed, to which nearly a third of the local children went. They were not hit by falling rolls as they could always be guaranteed their quota and know that their share of local children would increase as the overall population of secondary pupils reduced. This pushed their share of the pupils to near 30% in the 1990s.
2. two church schools which could attract pupils from across Thanet.
3. six secondary modern schools which had defined catchment areas. When there were empty places, pupils could be admitted from further afield.

The Conyngham School was always viewed as drawing on the most disadvantaged estates, although there were periods when other schools were also candidates for the 'bottom of the pile' spot.

The label, 'a school in challenging circumstances' (SCC) emerged in the 1990s. It was further subdivided to identify 'schools facing extremely challenging circumstances' (SFECC). It is worth thinking about these terms, which were not devised with the intention to blame or shame. However, the implication of both terms is that the origins of any problems lie in factors outside the school, perhaps with the culture of the community and families' disregard for education. Causal factors for a school underperforming are shared across the staff of a school, the community it serves and politicians' decisions. It raises again the question of how a society allows poor communities to exist, allows their children to go short of so many things including stimulation and school preparation, and allows schools to be insufficiently funded to deal with the educational needs of the children in the locality. Poverty, youth disillusion, bad schools and entrenched social ills are political issues where choices have been made *not* to intervene sufficiently strongly to meet needs. But the school was not in extremely challenging circumstances during its first two decades. Certainly it was not viewed as warranting that extreme label then.

A LITTLE BIT OF HISTORY

The Conyngham (pronounced Cunningham) school was built beside the estates which it was created to serve. Figure 4.1 shows it in glittering 1963 newness. The Conyngham family owned large tracts of land between Canterbury and the Thanet coast which included coalfields and the land upon which both the estates and the school were built. A representative of the family, the Earl of Mount Charles, came to open the school in January 1963 and the school was permitted to use the family name and even incorporate the pitchfork, like a capital 'Y', from the family coat of arms into the school badge. The school's motto on the badge is 'Steadfast'.

Figure 4.1. Conyngham School 1963.

Within a decade, Conyngham had become a tough working class school. The name changed to The Ramsgate School in 1996, shortly before its new name was blazoned across the local and national press as 'the worst school in England', which happened in 1997, and again in 2003. In the period from 1996 to 2005, The Ramsgate School struggled to lift its performance, and eventually underwent a radical transformation of buildings and funding in 2005 to become The Marlowe Academy, a new school but one which still had to work hard to provide a suitable quality of education.

The history of the school can be divided into four periods, largely determined by national developments. The first two periods are chronicled in this chapter. The first period sees the Conyngham School as a decent, well-enough respected secondary modern doing the best it could for those in the local area. This was the secondary modern of quiet, untroubled and private satisfaction and lasted until around1992. The second period was a time of stress, strain and public turbulence when the National Curriculum, Local (financial) Management of Schools and league tables constrained the school and told the world how poorly it performed. The school's problems intensified during the 1990s. The third period from 1999 until 2005 (Chapters 5 and 6) was the period of interventions and attempted rescues as the school 'bumped along the bottom'. The fourth and last period (Chapters 7 and 8) is about establishing the new school, its community ethos as an academy and consolidating its work with the children, parents and community.

In the 1960s, secondary modern schools were generally seen as the place for working class children, and were the most numerous type of school found all over the country, each one very much a reflection of its neighbourhood. Although in 1965 the government issued its famous circular 11/65 that encouraged the creation of comprehensive schools, in 1966 John Partridge[8] could still write, 'children are selected at eleven years of age for differing types of school, and hence for differing occupational opportunities'. That was the class-based nature of the system even if disguised as a meritocracy. There was an inbuilt inequality which the comprehensive system was designed to break down and, by the mid 1970s, all but 36 local authorities had gone comprehensive. Nevertheless, Kent retained its grammar schools, three of which were in Thanet. In theory, the tripartite system (grammar, technical and secondary modern) continued to prevail, but a dearth of Technical Schools effectively created a bipartite system.

From 1981, Scotland introduced free-market approaches to education, the idea being that it increased competition among schools and required school staff to become more accountable to parents. Critics were concerned that school choice may increase the segregation of students with differing backgrounds and would not necessarily improve the performance of schools.

Later, the 1988 Education Reform Act introduced this approach in England. The same worries were voiced about whether this would lead to greater polarisation in the social composition of schools. Similar concerns were expressed about the changes proposed in the 2005 *Higher Standards, Better Schools for All* White Paper which became the Education and Inspections Act 2006. It placed emphasis on greater parental choice and greater independence for schools. The 2010 coalition government's hasty first Education white paper continued the trend to free schools from local authorities and allowed different sorts of schools to emerge. Social segregation is so often a consequence of such developments.

In most areas of England, secondary school selection arrangements are further complicated by the existence of church schools and the established pecking order of high schools. Up to the 1990s, where school choice was limited and the education markets had not really got under way, church schools were just another type. When school choice was opened up, the view was that parents would reject the bad schools and cause them to either improve or close. But markets can serve the sellers, the providers of education in this case. Some argue that entry requirements enable denominational education providers to erect barriers to entry that tacitly sieve out the needy and deprived by using religious affiliation as a proxy for social class. In so far as this is true, a consequence is that location, history or reputation will nail some schools to the bottom. These are the ones labeled 'failing schools', 'schools in challenging circumstances', often schools in 'special measures' and 'national challenge schools'. Once publicly in this position, secondary schools often find it hard to improve their standing. The story of Conynham School which became The Ramsgate School and then the Marlowe Academy provides an example of this condition, this struggle and this inequity.

PERIOD ONE: SOCIAL BACKGROUND AND HISTORY OF THE CONYNGHAM SCHOOL – THE DECENT, RESPECTED SECONDARY MODERN FROM 1963–1992

The Conyngham School opened as an 11–16 secondary modern school in 1963. It was the first new secondary school to be built in Thanet for 50 years. It cost £141,500 and was intended to relieve pressure on other secondary modern schools in the district. The local newspapers spoke optimistically about the school's future and the inaugural speech by the headmaster was grandiose in its thanks and expectations, 'To the policy-makers and the planners may I say you have given us a fine building in the modern idiom as befits the materials of which it is made.' There were just eight teachers for the 120 pupils. A former teacher from that era reported 'They were happy days. The head wanted to provide the children with facilities, so we had a swimming pool and a croquet lawn'.

The mines were still open and Newington was, to a substantial extent, a mining estate containing about 40% mining families. In the 1960s, over 5,000 miners worked in the four Kent pits, all of which were in the east of the county close to Thanet. But changes loomed. A report in the local newspaper in December, 1963 was headlined 'TEENAGE JOBLESS: OVER 3,600 HIT.' In 1969, Chislet colliery, operating since 1914, closed. Up to this point, Newington had existed as a working class estate with wage earners, a dignity in labour and probably a widespread view that school mattered little, but you had to go there.

While the period of relatively full employment persisted, Newington was reported as a decent estate with hard-working families. The memory of a very young vicar on the estate in the late 60s was that 'Newington did not come across as a poor estate then, as it does now'. The bulk of the estate were miners, mostly from Wales, 'pretty rough but the majority, all those who came to the church, were lovely people. It was tough but most had hearts of gold when you got to know them'. He recalled, 'delightful children, some of whom would baby-sit for my young family'.

Schools in former coalfield areas register high on many of the indicators of deprivation associated with schools in challenging circumstances, although research suggests that these areas and their problems do not have some particular 'coal miners' culture' dimension. Newington became a 'former mining' area in 1989 with the closure of the last of the Kent pits. The bitterness of the miners' strike of 1984/85 remained long after the strike was over, leaving a legacy of antagonism between striking and working miners that some say is still present between families and even within families. One pupil at the time recalls striking miners' wives at the gate pelting the children of working miners with eggs and working miners' children being taught separately for a while 'for their own safety'. Senior staff of the time remember no such effects of the strike on the school, but folk memories are notoriously inconsistent.

Mr S – Headteacher 1

The first head teacher of the Conyngham School in 1963, Mr S, came from Old Marston School in Oxfordshire, and remained as head until 1980. He brought with him a House system with prefects, tutorials and option afternoons on a Wednesday with non-academic activities. Mr S was described as 'the powerhouse behind the running of the school'. Close to his retirement, the 1980 issue of the school's Conyngham Magazine refers to '… the dominant theme of Mr S's education policy of caring for the individual – the clever, the less able, the shy, the forward, the strong and the physically handicapped'.

The accommodation was very generous while pupil numbers were still increasing, and it was a very busy, happy school. There is a 1965 picture of children and Mr S in swimwear with their feet dangling in the swimming pool under the heading of 'Do It Yourself Pool Opens.' But by 1970, pupil numbers approached 800 in a school built for 600. Teaching took place in the corridors, anywhere and everywhere. For one teacher, that was really the cause of the rapid decline in discipline. New buildings and further alterations from 1972 to 1974 increased capacity to 950 places, intending to cater for the raising of the school leaving age (ROSLA) in September 1972, natural growth, and development into a 13–18 comprehensive – which never happened.

Until well into the 1970s, the school was settled and regarded as satisfactory 'if rough'. A teacher who was there at the time recalled, 'It was an amiable era and the teachers in the school were very involved with the pupils and with their parents. It was like being part of a family'. It reportedly attracted good teachers at that time. Apparently, the head of maths co-authored a maths teaching scheme for less academic pupils, and two English teachers published stimulating lesson material for Conyngham-type children. Pupils from the first two decades report fairly positively and one girl, who joined the school in 1966, recalls overcoming her devastation at *not* making it to the grammar school, as 30 others from the estate primary school had done. She said that, 'It [Conyngham] was a state of the art school. It was absolutely fantastic. It was the most wonderful place you could imagine. At the end of year 1, I was asked if I wanted to transfer to the grammar school but I said no because I was so happy there'.

In terms of achievement, most years one or two children moved on to grammar school for A levels and, in September 1975, The East Kent Times reported that,

'14 pupils of Conyngham school at Ramsgate are celebrating their GCE results this week. Between them they chalked up 45 passes in 12 subjects. In the CSE exams the school totted up 443 passes in 20 subjects' There was no judgemental comment only vague praise with no sense of what it would be reasonable to expect in terms of CSE passes for a school of this type.

By the late 1970s, Conyngham was already a challenging school to teach in: some ex-pupils self-reported being 'unteachable and rude'. And parents were beginning to avoid the school if they were from outside the area. Locals who attended other Thanet secondary schools said they anticipated sporting fixtures against Conyngham with trepidation, such was its tough reputation. Yet those who went on to further and higher education appreciated the help they had received from some very committed teachers. Others who moved on to employment with few qualifications did not view the school as directly holding them back. Challenges were building through the first 16 years, but were burbling and murmuring rather than erupting. When Mr S retired in 1980 in poor health the school had over 1,000 pupils and those who knew him at the time recognised the stresses that running a large school in a working class area entailed.

Mr D – Headteacher 2

The second head teacher, Mr D, came from a nearby secondary school where he had been deputy, and was head of the school for 14 years from 1980, during which time a decline in pupil numbers accompanied a general deterioration in the school's fortunes. Pupil numbers were falling in the local primary schools but, by this time, Conyngham was firmly entrenched as a dumping ground for pupils excluded from other schools. It became less popular, even locally, and efforts were made to avoid sending children there if there was any claim to another school's catchment area. Some local primary school heads reportedly talked Conyngham down and councillors were also said to have spoken negatively about it.

The views of pupils who were at the school during this period are varied, but a majority stated that it was possible to do OK so long as they worked with the teachers. Some described instances of bad teaching. Others found the increasing employment of supply teachers disrupted their learning. Pupils also reported boredom and irrelevance. They wanted 'less copying and more brain work'. Many pupils showed a willingness to learn, some even called for a special unit for disruptive pupils, but the reports also revealed a distinctly utilitarian outlook on learning. Pupils invariably did better in courses with a vocational application rather than humanities subjects or languages. The less committed voted with their feet. In 1985–6, attendance in the 3rd. year (Year 9) was around 85%, and in the Spring term, the term before the final examinations and assessments, 5th year (Year 11) average attendance was under 70%.

In many pupils' comments there are some enigmatic reflections tinged with self-doubt and self-blame. The following quotations are typical:

- I suppose that in some respects it was fairly good. If you tried hard they would support you. I was entered for eight CSEs but I didn't do very well. I had lost interest.
- There was a deterioration in years four and five (now Y10 and 11), in me and in them. Teachers were being ignored and they were ignoring the kids. Some did not teach. It seemed like the teachers had lost interest in the pupils.
- The bullying was unbelievable, but in lessons I could just sit there and get on with my work.
- It was what you made of it. You could work or be a dosser. I got five or six GCSEs.

By contrast, a pupil entering the school in 1990 had only negative things to say about the school, but acknowledged uncertainty as to how much was due to her, and how much was due to the staff. She reported that:

By the time I was 13 it was all over. It was the culture of the school, constantly disruptive. That's how we got our kicks. Lessons were constantly disrupted. I was a lost cause by then. I wasn't doing my work, I was always being sent out, on report. The predominant culture was disruption, violence and drugs. How can you learn in that environment when you are high on drugs or wanting to see how fast you could make the teacher lose his rag.

Mr D asserted that there were no drugs in the school as far as he could remember but the nearby car park beneath flats was a place which worried staff and there was certainly glue sniffing (but probably much more) until they got the council to block it up.

The staffing numbers, particularly the number of support staff, were much lower than in the present day Marlowe Academy, and most other secondary schools in 2011–12. In the 1980s and early 90s the number of teaching and support staff varied from around 40 teachers and 15 additional staff in 1985 with 660 pupils, to around 38 teachers and 17 support staff for 580 pupils in 1986–7. The non-teaching staff numbers included secretaries, technical assistants, caretakers, canteen and lunchtime supervisors, plus welfare assistants and special services staff – principally for a small number of disabled students. Roughly a third of the teachers were aged over 45, a third had been there over 15 years, mostly the heads of department and heads of house. But absenteeism rose to nearly a fifth of the staff on some days putting strain on other staff, 'the increase probably as much associated with exhaustion or stress than with other illness'. Supply teachers were not easy to find, and had to be looked after if they were to be able to cope and return when needed.

The school had a flourishing vocational curriculum up to the 1990s with a rural studies unit, hair dressing and car maintenance. The main body of pupils was divided 50:50 into upper and lower ability half year groups, referred to as 'Ac' (Academic) and 'Voc' (Vocational) respectively. The school had been enthusiastically involved with the Technical and Vocational Educational Initiative (TVEI) and Young Enterprise, had a very successful work experience programme and had developed strong links with Thanet Technical College. However, the change to Local Management of Schools meant that the school, rather than the LEA, had to pay, and the school felt it could no longer afford these extra links.

Mr D acknowledged that, 'The primary priority was control, keeping things under control. There were fights and some quite unpleasant stuff'. Discipline was a continuing worry. One senior teacher wrote of the concern over discipline which 'forces teachers to adopt control strategies with some classes which aimed more at containment and survival than genuine education. Thus, the completion of simple repetitive tasks and rote copying are used as a means of control and of minimizing the risks of exciting the disruptive pupil'. Though involved in much curriculum development of the time, there was little appetite for the more adventurous approaches to teaching, or 'brain work' as the pupil put it.

Mr D enjoyed very good personal relationships with officers in the divisional education office who supported him. 'They were the good old days when everything was controlled from the district office – none of your local management which came in big time after I left – so one could always blame the local office for your problems'. Parents' evenings were always well-attended and always friendly.' He had never been threatened with physical violence. 'There was always, every day, some child who would need some very explicit disciplinary intervention.' There was a system for misbehaviour in the classroom and a room outside the head's office was used to contain children sent out – 'only three or so a day given detention'.

Although Mr D could recall no pupil moving to grammar school to take GCEs from the Conyngham, as with any school of that type in that era, people could point to successes – pupils who went off to teacher training college, a small number who got 'A' Levels either at the grammar schools or Thanet Tech where they went after their GCSEs or gained qualifications later. It did not seem to be the case that experience at the school had merely pandered to any pupil lack of aspiration, contributed to under-achievement or blighted lives. This may be accurate in relation to those who wanted to work. But teachers who worked there through the 1980s did feel that the number of difficult children increased and that behavioural problems became more frequent and sustained. Staff from Canterbury Christ Church College, who supervised student teachers on teaching practice, recalled what a tough assignment it was for students. Some qualified teachers reportedly joined the school, became disappointed at what they were able to achieve, and left. Yet there were teachers who, like many pupils, reported being content while at the Conyngham.

One teacher provided this assessment:

> If you put it into perspective, you could see the limitations that the children actually lived with and that expectations were reasonable in relation to their families and situations. You needed to understand where the pupils came from. Talking with them you would understand their problems and at case conferences you would sometimes be amazed at their resilience in relation to what they had to put up with. Those were the reasons they were not achieving in education. They were not causing problems, not rebelling. There were families who came through the school who had huge difficulties and you could marvel at how they managed to function as well as they did.

Although education professionals understood the school's position and its problems, it was still possible to present a reassuring picture to others. The local newspapers in the eighties reported fairly positively about the school but that was a time when comparisons between schools and league table positions were not fed by data and advertised. The press would largely celebrate the positives handed to them by the school. Such media attention as was directed at the school and its staff, pupils and parents remained gentle and kindly. At a time when governors were expected to support, rather than challenge as is expected today, the school's governors appeared to share this positive perspective. The minutes of governors' meetings record oral reports of governors' visits, which were invariably positive, although they decreased in number over time as concern mounted about the cost of vandalism, levels of absenteeism and the use of exclusions.

PERIOD TWO: THE CONYNGHAM SCHOOL – EXPOSURE, COMPARISON, MARKETS AND DOWNWARD PRESSURES 1993–1999

Up to the early 1990s Conyngham School rolled along, certainly struggling with its challenges, but in a fairly undemanding national educational environment. Then a new era of imperatives and judgements came into play, intensifying the focus upon a school that was always the bottom of the pile, and multiplying Mr D's problems and stresses. From 1993, all secondary schools had to publish their examination results. Now everyone could examine and compare the performance of all schools, and the importance of GCSE attainment became nationally and locally significant.

The worries about pupil numbers and the vulnerability of being a small school in a big building continued, and now additional concerns over publicly exposed poor exam results pushed the school towards new levels of unpopularity. This increased the difficulties in the quest for more pupils and more staff. Until the early 1990s, as the school roll fell, there had been no rush for early retirement or redundancy. By 1992 there was more willingness to accept a deal especially as changes in early retirement conditions were imminent and school was becoming a more difficult environment for successful teaching. The head remarked on the meeting of heads to place pupils, 'The dreadful market place system where we decided what to do with those who were excess to requirements, so to speak. Well, I said, "Give them to me. I'll take anybody", and I meant that literally. Everything was based on numbers, [including] financial allocation, [and] staffing'.

Despite the problems and challenges, Mr D looked back on 'fourteen very happy years, tough years but not soul-destroying years' He valued the exciting curriculum developments they had been involved in, including TVEI with other local secondaries, the school trips, the partnership with a French school, and the way he had functioned as an old style head, 'always on duty at lunchtime, knew all the pupils by name, at the school gate when trouble was brewing and at the local sweet shop when complaints came through from there'. The school had lunch time and after school activities and, for a period of a few years, had a youth club based in it and ran a breakfast club.

He recognised that the Conyngham was always the bottom school and that there was room for only one reject school. He thought he and the staff had accommodated to the situation and on his departure in 1994 he felt, 'There was little more I could do. What we were doing matters a great deal, but I was a pragmatist. You make the best of what you've got. If we had 6–10% 5A-C GCSEs, it would be a miracle. I'm not joking. But it certainly wasn't merely survival, not sleepless nights.'

He did not realise that the results were so poor in comparison with other schools in the country until league tables appeared. He knew it surprised the local authority, staff, children, colleagues elsewhere and even parents. As another teacher said of these times, 'When league tables came in, in the early 90s, to begin with we did not take much notice. Later it became something that you could not ignore'. There was a local authority inspection in 1994 which was said to be 'fairly critical' and it is suggested that this – added to the market pressures and league table position – prompted Mr D's retirement in that year. The prospects were more of the same – more pressure.

Mr B – Headteacher 3

Table 4.1 shows the low levels of achievement of 5 GCSCs at grades A* – C during the years 1994 to 1999. While the table shows that achievement was undeniably very low, it also shows that the percentage of pupils eligible for free school meals stood at over 50% against the contemporary national average of around 13%. This indicates that the proportion of children from low income families in the school was four times the national average. Furthermore, at levels from 45% to 72%, the proportion of pupils on some level of the special educational needs (SEN) register was very, very high when compared to the national average of 18%. Cognitive Abilities Test (CAT) scores on entry at 11 (not shown in the table) were correspondingly low. But the mood of the times was not to make allowance for any extenuating circumstances. In the eyes of politicians and the media, achievement was now the sole criterion of a school's success.

Table 4.1. GCSE attainment, numbers on Roll, SEN and FSM 1993–1999

	The Conyngham/Ramsgate School				Nationally
Year	*Number on Roll*	*% 5A*-C GCSEs*	*% Special Educational Needs*	*% Free School Meals*	*% 5A*-C GCSEs*
1994	477	1	45	50	*43*
1995	445	1	56	50	*43*
1996	408	1	65	50	*44*
1997	378	1	71 (inc 29 statements)	51	*45*
1998	542	10	71	50	*46*
1999	560	7	72 (inc 34 statements)	55	*47*

Mr B took over as acting head in 1994 having previously been the deputy, and in 1996 had the name changed to The Ramsgate School, to give it a sense of place. He had been delighted to get the headship, 'It was not "Oh my god, what have I taken on?"'. He knew all the Thanet secondary head teachers, their perceptions of the school and their expectations of its role. He detected some suspicion from these colleagues about whether he would challenge these expectations, and this was especially evident 'at the divvying up ceremony for new entrants, about whether I would play my part reasonably': as the school of last resort which would receive pupils they did not want. He was largely content to fit in and indeed had little option.

In 1997, the school hit the national headlines for the first time as 'the worst school in England', a school with 1% passes at GCSE level at a time when the national average was 45%. The national press interviewed the head teacher and nothing that could be said would set aside the stark low attainment figures. The press was camped outside the school all week so Mr B invited them in and was open with explanation and upbeat with plans for the future; that was not how it was treated in The Sun, The Times and especially The Sunday Times. He recalls, 'I felt damaged by that'. This was the definitive first blast of punishing and unforgiving negative publicity which was a blow for every teacher in the school.

Their first Ofsted inspection that year had categorised the school as having 'serious weaknesses', and the school was then really exposed through the new combined pressures of league tables, SATs, local management of schools and parental choice of school. Because the school had space, ever higher numbers of children with additional needs were being funnelled into the school, either because they had been rejected elsewhere, were newcomers to the area or had been excluded from other schools. There was an increase in the numbers in the care of the local authority and in students from eastern Europe, some of whom in both categories were seriously damaged, having witnessed awful happenings. In 1998, numbers leapt as one secondary school was closed and most of its children came to The Ramsgate School. The school no longer seemed to be the Newington estate's local school. Its pupil population now came from many places within Thanet.

The 1997 inspection report emphasised the very low proportion of children achieving five or more GCSEs at A* to C, the same 1% level as in each of the previous three years. The report stated: 'These results are not satisfactory. The high proportion of pupils who do not attend regularly is a major factor in accounting for the poor A* to C pass rate. How far short the school fell of the national average was brought home by the tables of 1996 results at Key Stage 3 and Key Stage 4 where the proportion achieving at the higher levels in English, maths and science was negligible compared to the national average of one-quarter to one-third. Pupils performed better than the average nationally in the diploma of vocational education. But overall, the report painted a gloomy picture of pupils' experience and achievement in the 136 lessons observed.

The report recorded several factors that clearly contributed to low achievement in the school: 'on entry to the school, the attainment of most pupils is very low compared to the national average', and it was noted that over half the children were entitled to free school meals, 71% of pupils had some level of special educational need, and that unemployment in the area was twice the county average. No attempt was made to explain to readers how these factors should be taken into account.

Looking at such a critical report, it is highly relevant to consider the malign influence of the three grammar schools that creamed off over 30% at the top of the pupil ability range from the school's catchment area, but the Ofsted report did not do so. Nor did it acknowledge the similar competition for an able pupil intake coming from faith schools and other high schools in more favoured locations. The implication is that the school should – somehow – make itself equally attractive as these other schools to parents and pupils. An important argument advanced in this book is that it is not at all a reasonable expectation.

The Ofsted report's publication in 1997 marked a new low point and one which the head and staff worked hard to improve on. Head teachers did not see The Ramsgate School as 'a different animal', as one put it, but just as a school with some greater problems. More support was offered by the County Council via the county's support team offering advice and the availability of a small amount of extra money.

Mr B calculated that resources available to support failing schools were negligible at that time; the levels of differentiation in funding were not sophisticated then, though they received significantly extra funding from their special needs count. He knew that ministers took an interest in the most challenging schools and he went by invitation to see Stephen Byers, then a junior minister in education. He went with a KCC officer, the local MP and, with his 'shopping list,' intent on getting additional support. The minister simply bounced this back as a local authority responsibility and he got nothing extra – not from the LA, nor from central government. That is how he remembers it. Other papers suggest that around this time an additional £20,000 would be granted to schools in this predicament. This was a trivial amount in relation to evident needs, which Mr B put at £500,000, especially as the turnover of staff was beginning to increase alarmingly. In September 1998, a third of the staff was new to the school.

An Ofsted team returned two years later in 1999 and judged that the school could come out of serious weaknesses. Even then the results at Key Stage 3 and in GCSE examinations were 'very low.' In their report, while the inspectors praised the good ethos for learning, sound leadership and satisfactory resources and behaviour, they pointed to unsatisfactory planning and timetabling and, 'the school still does not quite provide satisfactory value for money'. But achievement had risen strongly: 10% of pupils achieved five A to C grades compared with the 1% two years earlier, and indeed for the two years before that. At this second inspection, a local head was called to give evidence from a wider perspective. He said that one inspector remarked that it was the 'largest *special school* they had ever inspected'. The proportion of special needs pupils was extraordinary.

Whatever his motives, there was the feeling that the head teacher then moved, in September 1999, to a nearby school while the going was good. More generously, people recognised that Mr B had taken the school off the bottom of the league tables, increased the roll beyond just bringing in the pupils from the closed Holy Cross school, and shown the strengths that made him a good candidate for a larger school nearby. He was remembered as a head always out and about in the school. The joke was that his office was never used.

Mr B judged that he was leaving the school in good order with every possibility that it would prosper if determinedly and energetically led. This was to disregard the drop in popularity with parents. Only 10% of 11 year olds from the two local primary schools were opting to come to the school. Staffing problems were increasing, fewer teachers were teaching exclusively their main subject, the threat of bad publicity for your workplace and the damage to one's professional reputation had already been vividly and painfully experienced and there was a shrugging acceptance that there were 'limits to what you could do with these children' that was deeply embedded. Mr B also reflected on the reputation of the estate: 'When you talk to people in other areas, they talk about it as a no-go area, you don't want to go there, but people living there don't feel that way. The external view is dreadful, but there is some sense of community in some parts'. Many would say the estate was not as bad as its reputation. Nor was the school: just as some pupils loved it, so did some staff: 'In all my years of teaching there at The Ramsgate School (1989–97) I loved it. It broke my heart to leave. I sobbed'.

ENDNOTE

The optimistic view of one local commentator was that The Ramsgate School was at a point where it could go in a number of directions: 'build up, building on and taking forward what had been achieved after a successful Ofsted', partnering with a better regarded local secondary (maybe an idea ahead of its time) or to go down the route of independence to academy status.

A primary head said that 'Parents would have sent their children ANYWHERE but to The Ramsgate School. The Ramsgate School had to pick up the pieces. Other heads were content that The Ramsgate School existed and had places. There was little support from other schools. A sink school does them all favours by soaking up the more challenging kids, those new to the area and those who can't find a place in another school'. The Ofsted report for 1999 showed an increase in the percentage with 5 A-C GCSE passes to 10% and set a target for the next year of 15%; in the event it was 7%. Two years later it was 3% and its reputation plummeted further. Strong leadership had managed to hold the fort and improve things steadily, but that leadership had left.

The period from 1963 to 1993 could be viewed as an era that ended with the arrival of the national curriculum, league tables, local management of schools, Ofsted inspections and the pressure to 'perform.' It was an era in Thanet when, despite most local authorities having 'gone comprehensive' nearly thirty years previously, the secondary modern schools were still expected to thrive. It was, however, also a period when youth unemployment had set in, when unskilled and semi-skilled jobs became harder to find and when qualifications really did make a difference to obtaining a job or not. So we had the beginnings of Period Two for the Conyngham School, characterised by a battle which grew in intensity, a battle to which schools at the bottom of the heap had not previously been exposed, and which they were ill-equipped to fight.

In the period 1993 to 1999, problems of every sort were becoming entrenched and very soon after 1999, it became clear that the school was not 'building up, building on and going forward'.

THE WORST SCHOOL IN ENGLAND –
WHOSE FAULT?

INTRODUCTION

This chapter documents the way the school descended into the bottom category of schools. It reports attainment results, pupil numbers, pupil and staff turnover, national and local press comment, and the views of teachers and local people as The Ramsgate School went through a turbulent time as a *school in extremely challenging circumstances.*[9] At the core of this and the next chapter is an account of the four attempts to support and improve the Ramsgate School until it became the Marlowe Academy in September, 2005. Later in this book, in Chapter 9, these attempts are put into the national context where failing schools, or national challenge schools, are most often found in the country's more deprived areas where they struggle with a range of disadvantages beyond the entry characteristics of the incoming children, but with levels of additional funding that are never sufficient to compensate.

In this third period of the school's existence, the school was exposed to public view as never before, and its reputation was dire in the immediate local area, across the county and nationally. In 1999 the head teacher of five years moved on to the headship of a neighbouring secondary school and, thereafter, The Ramsgate School had a series of leadership appointments, brokered by the local authority, whose efforts to support the school increased yearly:

- 1999–2000: Mr K was seconded for one year from the Boys' grammar school
- 2000–2002: Ms G, from a headship in Kent, was appointed on a two year contract
- September 2002 – May 2003: Mr N, from a headship in Kent, to a permanent appointment
- April 2003 (takeover from May) – August 2005: Mr H, executive head and a team of four (Chapter 6)

In August 2005, The Ramsgate School closed and in September The Marlowe Academy opened under a new principal, a new senior management team, and with approaching 50% new staff (Chapter 7).

At the start of this period, when the school had come out of serious weaknesses and staff were thrilled, all was not as good as was made out. One Kent senior education officer said that when the re-inspection took place in May 1999, 'If I had been the registered inspector, I would have put it in special measures. It was a mistake to take it out. We did a good job flannelling them. Staff reacted in thinking all was now well. It wasn't'.

OVERVIEW OF THE PERIOD

During these four years, attainment levels for the first four years were stubbornly rock bottom, (See table 5.1), remaining at about one tenth of those prevailing nationally. From 2002 to 2005 the numbers on roll fell by 180 children, over a quarter. Being in special measures, the school had some powers to limit the admission of new arrivals to the area, especially pupils excluded from other local schools. In the early period, no two or five year plans appeared to be in place to break through these very low attainment levels, or more generally to address the poor educational provision which lay behind these figures.

Table 5.1. GCSE attainment, SEN and FSM 2000–2005

	The Ramsgate School				Nationally		
Year	Number on Roll	% 5A*-C GCSEs	% Special Educational Needs	% Free School Meals	% 5A*-C GCSEs	% Special Educational Needs	% Free School Meals
2000	597	3	55 (inc 7% statements)	36	49	18	15
2001	626	4	44 (inc 9% statements	36	50	19	14
2002	653	4	38 (inc 5% statements	37	52	18	15
2003	648	4	44 (inc 5% statements)	34	53	15	15
2004	552	15	48	31	54	16	14
2005	470	18	59	36	56	17	14

Mr K – Headteacher 3

There had been interviews for the post of headteacher in the Summer of 1999, but no appointment was made. The new headteacher in September 1999, was Mr K, a senior teacher from a local grammar school who was to have been the deputy seconded in and linked for one year with a headteacher from another Thanet secondary school in a partnership arrangement. This never worked because that school's governors would not release him.

Mr K was not keen to begin with, but owned to being tempted by 'a challenge worth trying in the twilight years of my career.' He admitted to being an odd choice with 'a curiously different background', with no knowledge of special needs, no experience at all of a difficult school and whose joy had been teaching scholarship physics. There was no financial advantage to him until a £4,000 increase at Christmas, but that was still an estimated £20,000 less than the headteacher who followed him. He went in on the understanding from the county officer that there would be support. But it was strange that the county, local officers or the governors should entrust the school to a teacher with Mr K's background. This was half the original plan and patently inadequate.

Mr K knew the school from the 1970s and 80s because the Jackey Baker field beside the Conyngham, was where his school used to come for games. He remembers the pupils 'used to come and interrupt our games and shout abuse from the side-lines. That slightly colours your view as these characters seemed to be ill-disciplined compared with the grammar school boys I was supervising'. He had visited the school for the 11+ panel meetings which were often held at the Conyngham, 'and it was well-behaved, calm not a seething hotbed of discontent'.

When Mr K arrived at the school he found it fully staffed in graffiti-free buildings that were in fairly good order with reasonable space – even if there was a lot of asbestos and ill-fitting windows. As for the low academic attainment, as Mr K saw it, 'I don't think that league tables applied to these children. It makes them feel failures when the bar is always too high for them.' The school had earlier had other facilities and courses which appealed to these children, motor mechanics, hairdressing and a farm. The national curriculum pressures pushed these out. 'It ended up making the secondary high schools in Kent imitations of the grammar schools and it does not work'. He thought he understood the limitation of the curriculum for these children before arriving at the school, and was quickly convinced that, 'the education diet they were getting was entirely inappropriate, because, to be quite honest, trying to get them to speak French when they are struggling with English makes no sense at all'.

The decision to take the post was made on the basis that there would be support, 'because it was a hefty thing to do on your own.' However, 'going in solo', Mr K actually found himself, 'abandoned in the first term apart from the occasional visit or a phone call asking, "Everything all right, then?"'. He 'waded in,' but felt that he was never given any great clarity, and the responsibility was thrown onto the shoulders of well-meaning governors when he needed support based on professional experience.

Wisely, he did not go in with *a vision* but said to the staff that he would have to find out what the school was all about. His first challenging question was: How can anyone teach children like this, when they're behaving like this? 'Because there's no point in sorting out their educational needs until you have sorted out the social side first.' He recalled that some, including those who came later, said, 'Provide the right education and they will fall into line'. Providing the right education did not happen in his view and probably did not in the years immediately after his departure. It needed something more radical.

He wanted to raise the level of behaviour, get the children into school uniform, and get them to be polite to staff. He ate with them. It was like Alcatraz when he started, with food being thrown across the room. He put a stop to that. He felt the main vehicle to reach pupils was through assemblies and he used to tell them stories with a moral. He did not think this had happened before. While staff too appreciated his style, he did have a member of staff say after one assembly that it was all very nice but not only was it over the heads of the children but it was over hers as well. But they listened respectfully and in silence. He also tried to get to know all the pupils who were really disruptive, talk to them. Behaviour was surprisingly better than he thought.

The words Mr K used were, 'docile, lethargic, surprisingly biddable but they were undernourished to look at. They were not difficult kids, but kids who were made to be difficult'. His own approach was to lower his voice and talk to them 'rather than shout at them because they were always getting shouted at'. Discipline elsewhere in the school was loud and forceful, if inconsistent, and staff used fixed term exclusions too frequently.

His second challenge was finding half way through the first term that the budget was in deficit by over £100,000. It placed a limit on what he could do but, worse still, the county insisted that he had to cut staff. Yet he needed more staff. 'It was like having the rug pulled'. The deficit was vaguely attributed to lost income from a project, which did not happen, and/or funds not following children from a school that was closed the previous year. He did not reconsider his position. He thought some economies could be made, but in the end just got on with it. Whatever happened, Kent County Council was not going to close the school. To compound this challenge, the bursar and site manager had resigned at the same time as the departing head. New people were appointed and efforts made to market the school more to attract pupils and their accompanying revenue.

A third area of challenge was staff, organisation and management. He was aware that some were strong teachers and others very weak. Some lesson content and delivery was inappropriate and he could see why pupils got bored. He observed a lot of lessons each week and wanted to support some development and improvement, 'but I seemed to be solo in all this.' For other senior management it seemed to be a fire brigade role, intervening in problems all around the school, dealing with a child misbehaving, sending children home.' He felt he had competing tensions and what was right for the children and what was right for the staff were not the same, 'The staff were in survival mode'. A school like that needed the best teachers, most highly motivated and most highly paid, 'not teachers who percolate to the bottom of the heap because they can't get in anywhere else'. There was a shrill atmosphere with senior management always rushing around. Their weakness was lack of confidence. Some senior staff taught very little and seemed to look after themselves. The lack of support available internally and from outside led Mr K to complain to the county officer who had appointed him and he brought in a deputy from another school 'who was good, a whirlwind, but confrontational'.

On one day, 11 staff were off sick out of 38 and amongst these was the senior teacher who organised cover. On a later occasion 16 out of 40 were missing. He tried to get collegiality with morning briefings. He encouraged some good staff development, sat in on departmental meetings and wanted to support people. He encouraged them to take on tasks, 'but so often they did not get done so you ended up doing them yourself'. Even deadlines for pupil assessments were missed with, 'Oh, I'll get them in next week'.

Mr K found the special needs department running a school within a school and with the department head on maternity leave, there was resistance to change. He would have changed it if he had been there longer. There was said to be 70% SEN but in his view it was probably nearer 40%. That was an excuse for how poorly the pupils performed. 'I felt all the time that they were making excuses. The special needs area was dour and controlled, without a sense that things could improve. By the second term, Mr K was able to reflect realistically that the school should not have been taken out of serious weaknesses, a judgement endorsed by his deputy, newly seconded in.

This was undoubtedly a difficult year and Mr K worked hard as the lone leader to manage behaviour, raise morale and achieve better results. He lost two and a half stone in weight and did not sleep much for a whole year. The experience clearly took its toll and people said he looked 'hollowed out'. He was there daily from 7 am sometimes until 8 pm and was busy the whole day. He was out every evening seeing that the pupils getting on the bus behaved themselves. He would check with the bus driver in the morning to see how things had gone. He did lesson observations and individual consultation. He dealt well with parents and was around for after-school activities, though not many children stayed on for these. The job was relentless with no free-wheeling or times when you could drop your guard. But he stayed the year as contracted and then moved back to his grammar school position. He had not expected attainment results to improve; that was a five year plan during which they could get the behaviour right. This was a short-term appointment and in many respects he was getting the school ready for the next new head. Some of the problems were too deep-seated and conflict-laden for a one-year seconded head to tackle. He was asked if he wanted to stay on, but in the Autumn, when the financial issues had unexpectedly and unfairly erupted, he had decided that he would stick to the one year contract. There was a 30% staff turnover at the end of his year.

He felt very sad at the end of it and that, had he been younger, he could have done more. There was a moral purpose in him being there and people commented on his 'straightness and decency', but more than this was quite evidently needed. He had a warm send-off from staff and pupils. He did not complain about the pupils. He did not think their behaviour was at all outrageous and had seen worse in a grammar school. As he saw it, the pupils were not being offered a good educational deal and that provoked poor behaviour and strained relationships between pupils and staff. Mr K was underpowered from the outset, a lone leader without operational and strategic support from within the school or the LA. In addition, he was burdened by financial challenges. Nevertheless, the pupils had gained much from their 'value added'. Some of that was getting them to come to school, turn up on time, be properly dressed, stay the day, and behave reasonably. The school was a haven for many. But, he felt, in the end because the teaching staff's expectations became all too low, what the children achieved was all too limited. A summary judgement was that the school had not declined during the year, the line had been held.

Once again, despite two rounds of interviews, no appointment was made for the following year, which was a strong indication of the difficulty of finding the right person to lead The Ramsgate School out of its difficulties. It was made clear that

KCC would need to raise investment and the Head of the county's Special Support Team said this would be forthcoming. The seriousness of The Ramsgate School's position was now acknowledged not just at district level, but at county level. The Director of Education and the KCC chair of the education committee expressed the views that the number of sink schools in Kent was intolerable and an embarrassment. The Ramsgate School was the biggest embarrassment of all, and the biggest let-down for children attending a Kent school. The Head of the Special Support Team, who had reduced the numbers of Kent schools in serious weaknesses from 50 to 20 and the number in special measures from 27 to seven had a track record from which to argue that, 'Schools like The Ramsgate School will only improve if their results improve and they get the confidence of the local area to send their children there. By achieving that they will fill their places. This will not remove the "worst" children but dilute them'. This was an acceptance of the market place in education which, arguably, was never going to work with bottom placed schools expected to attract pupils away from competitors. This really was so much against the odds.

Mrs G – Headteacher 4

A local head, Mrs G, was invited to take over the school, 'offered the challenge', from September 2000 for a period of two years to turn it around and take it to a more acceptable level. Mrs G arrived from a successful school, 'given an offer I would have been mad to refuse. For the last two years of my teaching career, the effect on my pension would be pretty good'. Having turned one school around she did not think The Ramsgate School would be as difficult as it turned out to be. She knew how Mr K had suffered.

She was quite clear on her arrival that, 'the major problem is the under-achievement. Definitely. That's the one thing that would get everyone off the school's back.' In her second term, she said that the plan for her appointment to the school and what she was to do there was not well thought through and was, 'One of [KCC officer's name] 2 am ideas … a desperation project.' With three senior people including herself on two year contracts, none of whom had worked together before, it was too ad hoc.

The demands of fire-fighting were not helped when she was 'leaned on' to take 60 children in her first term who were out of school and in Thanet, some being new arrivals. Mrs G negotiated a staggered entry but, 'Admitting all those extra children was a big blow because we thought we could have probably sorted out reasonable stability [with those we had]. We admitted a lot last week and probably a third are in trouble already'. This was a situation where different LA officers have different responsibilities and do not coordinate. Satisfying the placement of children by one officer actually undermined the efforts of the LA school support officer.

The school was not in special measures or serious weaknesses during the year before Mrs G's headship, nor during the two years of her tenure, but many observers said that it would have been if it had been inspected. In fact, the note of the HMI visit in January 2001 was a restrained warning of difficulties ahead. HMI acknowledged the low levels of attainment on entry, special needs, free school meal rates, mobile pupil population, 'the demoralising impact of a poor local reputation' and the very low attainment at 16. The school was judged at that point to be 'well led and managed' and that, 'the LEA is providing well-judged support'. But the danger signals were present in the HMI report.

A teacher who had left in 1991 and returned to a senior management position in 2001 found the school most definitely more difficult.

> It had become much, much worse. The teaching and learning had deteriorated considerably. I had spent so long working at the Conyngham and had worked with some outstanding teachers (reels off a string of names) and there was a high level of camaraderie. We all supported one another and if someone was having difficulties we would all support that person.

In 2001 nearly all those outstanding teachers had gone. The standard of dress of teachers had got worse. Some wore inappropriate clothing which, she felt, carried through into the classroom and into their practice. She was 'horrified,' and felt that it was a 'Rag, Tag and Bobtail of staff'.

It was very much an embattled environment where people taught their lessons and scuttled back to their base, to the departmental kettle. The corridors and playgrounds were in the control of the children in all sorts of ways. Things were so bad that the school nearly lost its part in the training of teachers because there were too few good role models – 'which was true'.

From the LA's viewpoint, all the school improvement efforts were ultimately to prepare The Ramsgate for academy status, a plan originated by the new Director of Education who arrived in 2002, although at that time only *city* academies were being opened. The importance of the academy plan shaped what heads would do as that goal approached, and signalled that the school's fate was important at the highest levels in the county and in national government. The resources that the county would be willing to lay out in the run up to the new academy would be huge – but they would be released after Mrs G's departure.

For two years Mrs G worked to motivate staff and pupils. A number of senior teachers were seconded in to lift the staffing capability of the school. But by 2001–02 nearly half the staff were unqualified, trainees, classroom assistants or newly qualified. They were inexperienced and not competent in the management of the children or their national curriculum learning.

Mrs G had accepted the job as headteacher of the school but with no choice about whether she took anyone with her. It proved difficult to form an effective SMT. She was given a deputy whom she had always known as a likeable person, 'but our views on how you run things were totally different'. He left after a term and a half. Her favoured informal ways of working were frustrated by the lack of a good team.

After one attempt at a full school assembly that was close to unruly, such formal gatherings were conducted in smaller sections. It signified a further decline in control and confidence from the previous year when Mr K held successful assemblies. Behaviour was not under control and the collective capacity and determination to get a sense of order was weaker still. One of the senior seconded staff with the best of reputations asked to be released. As he describes it,

> It was making me ill, not knowing what was happening next. I started smoking again. Dreadful experience. Kids would trash classrooms. It was like a tsunami. The long term teachers managed by just looking after themselves, a culture of 'I'm all right, Jack', and some departments were able to keep things OK in their areas. To make it work, you need the troops on the ground. With another teacher there at that time we looked back on The Ramsgate School experience as *the worst days of our lives*.

As Mr K had found on his arrival, finance was 'in a dreadful mess' and it was difficult to see where the money had gone. The school had virtually no computers, yet all Kent schools had received significant IT investment. Mrs G spent all the money 'we could beg, steal or borrow' on obtaining 200 computers and classroom white boards. 'The kids would know "we haven't got what the other schools have got. How can they expect us to do well?" and it's true.' This was about showing the school cared about the quality of their education by providing good accommodation and equipment. But it was clear that they were not getting quality adult input to go with it.

She abolished the special needs department, judging that 'taking three or four children away and teaching them to read was having no impact on anything'. She knew that she made enemies, but that improved with retirements and people moving. She wanted to improve the children's self-image – and the staff's – because staff took the branding in the same way as the children. As a boost, she even employed a real chef to run the school kitchen.

The dysfunctional nature of the school even extended to relationships with governors and 'the press were awful. If the press had left us alone for six months things would have moved more quickly', but that would always be a forlorn hope. Mrs G had sought to change organisation and behaviour, but knew 'attainment was going to take a long time'. She attributed this to a long-standing lack of confidence in teachers, pupils and parents. She judged that the entry profile was not that different from the technology school up the road[10] but, 'the potential had been squashed out of the children early on'. The entry profile, in terms of literacy rates and KS 2 levels achieved by the 11 year olds on entry, was lower than for any other secondary school in Thanet.

Observations by the author at that time revealed a poor school with poor children performing poorly. The pupils were under-size and movement about the school was fractious in an atmosphere that was close to bullying. The quality of lessons was variable and lateness to lessons frequent. In some there would be insults called across the class. In one Year 10 class of 14 a video was watched and worksheets were handed out. But pupils' attention to the task was desultory and there was no discussion. Little was picked up from the last lesson with slim prospect of continuity planning for onward learning. A science session was received with attention and successful teacher-pupil interaction, although the teacher had to emphasise the consequences of missed work through absenteeism. In contrast, an English supply teacher had the experience of pupils walking in and out of the lesson, some talking out of the first floor window to pupils outside, and very little done by most pupils on the 'homophone' worksheet. Underlying so much that one saw was the absence of a sequence of learning, not that it mattered to most of the pupils nor, indeed, to the teachers.

Mrs G reported that she found the organisation 'pretty bad. Heads of department were not used to acting on their own initiative any more than senior staff were, and one who did have potential, 'did not have the people around him to carry it through. The staff were described as dispirited, feeling themselves to be failures who believed that there was little that you could do because these were Ramsgate children.

Mrs G found the parents supported the children, not the school, and that they too were demotivated and expected little from their school. She believed that, 'If you can change the behaviour of a few, others follow and maybe you can then attract a few more, better ones, if that is the right word, pupils with better motivation or better motivated parents'.

High points of her period of headship at the school were identified as many small positives: good relationships with non-teaching staff; minor achievements like opening up the entrance area, providing a decent staffroom for the staff and new computers for pupils; members of staff deciding to do things off their own initiative; children who volunteered to do things; and working on the academy bid.
A low point was:

> … the frustration of seeing what ought to be happening and none of it happening. Having heads of year take more responsibility for their year; making heads of department take more responsibility for their exam results. You felt you were battling all the time. Some of the things were real battles like painting walls and them getting grafittied, then painting them again until the kids gave up. Vandalism was horrendous. Escapism was horrendous because the site was so open and you could just walk out. You could not patrol it.

There were many changes Mrs G wanted to bring about, but high staff absenteeism, low morale and difficulties in getting these staff to step up for additional duties and involvement inhibited this. She expressed some sympathy for that position in that the job was hard enough as it was. 'I don't know what the solution was short of getting rid of all the staff and starting again, which I think the group who took over later tried to do'. People were not picking up the baton, were not responding, they would do their lessons and withdraw. 'There was not much devotion to duty by a lot of people you would expect it of. The staff room would be empty by 4pm. It's a long time since I worked in a place like that. There was a lack of team spirit'. At the end of her two years, Mrs G just did not feel that she had the energy to go on any longer.

Following the advice of a Kent inspector, her strategy for the last two terms was to arrange meetings at least one day a week away from school. Sometimes these meant she was working at home. 'It gave me that breathing space, because the energy required, when every step is a fight, I could not have done it any longer. The county were trying a sticking plaster when it needed an amputation! They did not think children were important enough'.

Mrs G reflected that some of us have had a privileged upbringing and education (just stable families and grammar school) and some have nothing in what is supposed to be an egalitarian society. Acknowledging the larger issues of poor, discredited and poorly supported communities, she remarked sadly on the fact that the potholes started a mile down the road, houses were boarded up, three generations who had not worked, and it was not just the school which was neglected. 'If I lived there, I am not sure I would achieve very much'.

Mr N – Headteacher 5

The review of the school's position and the pessimism about its prospects of becoming an academy led to the permanent appointment from September 2002, again from Kent, of the first head dubbed a 'superhead', although Mrs G had also heard herself referred to with that label.

As with Mrs G, Mr N came with a good track record. A public school education and Oxford preceded a teaching qualification and teaching in schools in the west country in deprived areas. A headteacher in Kent before he was 40, his last post for 11 years began with a declining school population of 400 pupils, and ended with a very popular school of nearly 1,000. He was a head who was used to success.

He let it be known that he was ready for another job, but the process of his appointment was as confused as with the two previous heads. He was offered the post at the very last minute, accepted and went in with what he thought was the support of the local authority. He started at The Ramsgate on a salary less than Mrs G's but considerably higher than he was on in his previous school. It was becoming clear that the county's school support team could do a little, like finding the headteacher to take up the role and fund a small number of senior staff, but it had a limited budget and constricted choice on what and how much it could do.

Briefings from county officers and Mrs G had been very open and presented key challenges, apart from behaviour and attainment, such as getting the governing body onside and dealing with splits in the staff. There was no mention of external support but he was told that he did not have to worry about a deficit in the budget, as long as it was kept respectable.

He wrote a paper on the changes he thought necessary and agreed it with the Schools Support Team manager. He submitted this to staff before his arrival, and organised team meetings and staff training sessions at the start of September. He had no new staff coming with him. Of the staff he inherited, 40% were unqualified and the vast majority of heads of department were very new to their role. He had a senior management team of eight who had a total of two years senior management team experience between them. To address this level of staff inexperience in a suitably rational way, he persuaded the county team to lend him an external person to deal with the unqualified teaching and support staff, and a second person to work with the heads of department while he dealt with the senior management team.

'Almost every cupboard I opened, skeletons fell out. The situation was massively worse than anyone had realised.' He had a number of away days, some at the weekend – 'you couldn't afford to be away from the building' – to try to get some systems in place. There were lots of visits from county personnel, including the most senior officers. Though the academy issue was not the explicit motivation for the visits, it must have played a part. He showed the situation as it was and he judged that 'it frightened them'. The District Schools Officer was then the nominated person to relate to the school, and she was in the school at least once a week.

He reported that he got the governors on side, and most of the staff with him, by convincing them that, 'here was a new guy who was going to roll his sleeves up and work at the problems with them'. The only two instructions he recalled from the county staff were that he 'must not think that being head of a school like this was all about being macho and sacking staff. You can't sack staff because there is no one to replace them'. He did not seem inclined anyway to take this route, but it contrasted with the action taken nine months later. The second 'instruction' had been to rehabilitate a deputy who could do more, and he felt he had done that.

Out of 600 pupils, at the highest they had 85 looked after children (children in local authority care) from 35 different LAs. They had asylum seekers, 15 different languages, children coming and going every week. In the way it is calculated, the school's pupil mobility was 120%, actually off the scale of the DfES graph. It was ludicrous how the school was operating. 'Any parent with a decent kid would get them out as soon as they could.'

However, there was no two year period to bring the school up to scratch for Mr N. Two months into his tenure, two HMI came into the school for two days. Mr N said, 'They were foul. They ripped the school apart. They said 40% of the teaching was satisfactory and the rest was not. They said the management systems were appalling. They were absolutely condemning of absolutely everything'. Everything pointed to being put into *special measures*. They just about exonerated him from blame, he felt, as he was new, and they could see the place had been falling apart for years. But the HMI visit and report clearly rang alarm bells in Kent CC.

Soon after his own appointment, the new Director of Education visited the school in the autumn of 2002, recalling,

It was the most dispiriting place I had ever been to. It was not just the low achievement, the exclusions or the bad behaviour but the whole infrastructure of the place. That place was so bad and so difficult it had to have something draconian on behalf of children. It was an indictment of the local authority because they had presided over the decline of the school, a whole range of headteacher appointments and a model of change that did not work and had sat back and did not ask what else we can do but continued with more of the same. Nothing was really radical enough to make a difference. No one was doing anything to make parents welcome in or confident about the school.

The future sponsor of the academy, Roger De Haan, also visited and was shocked – the state of the buildings, the rubbish everywhere, dirty windows, falling ceiling tiles, broken lavatory seats, but worst of all the teaching and the screaming at children. 'I had to ask myself how did the education authority and the governing body of the school let it get so bad .... The children were being let down. ... A very unhappy place'.

Four HMI returned in January 2003 for two days. They observed 48 lessons or parts of lessons, two year group assemblies and six registration sessions, and concluded that 'The school requires special measures, since it is failing to give its pupils an acceptable standard of education.' The head agreed with this assessment, but he had been there only one term; many would say an inspection at any time in the previous four years would have seen the school placed in special measures.

The inspection report detailed many failings, including: pupils' progress limited primarily by weakness in teaching ... [and] unsatisfactory behaviour; significant numbers of teachers were unable to manage the pupils' work and behaviour effectively because of their poor classroom organisational skills; and day-to-day management often disorganised and sometimes chaotic. Damning indeed, and the inspectors could reasonably have expected to see some of these issues confronted within the first term of a new headteacher. The key issues identified in the HMI's report were banal[11]: requirement that the school raise attainment, reduce unsatisfactory teaching, improve the effectiveness of leadership and establish a learning culture. All this was obvious and the inability of the school to do it was precisely why it was in this state.

At this point the local authority completely lost faith in the capacity of the school, under Mr N's leadership, to respond to these issues and bring it to a position where an application for academy status could be responsibly made. Becoming an academy while still performing very poorly was not ruled out, but the thinking generally was that the handing over should be done when the school was in better order. The Director was by this time worried and saw the possibility of the millions to fund the solution to the school being lost.

Mr N was asked to draw up an action plan and present it to a group at County Hall in 10 days, a most unusual request for a headteacher. It signified the priority given to the school at the highest levels. It was obvious that his presentation was not well received. He did not get the support he wanted and got the message that the authority was not pleased, 'and that came from the top'.

What was galling for Mr N was that, as the headteacher who had gone in with their blessing, and not being particularly helped by the County, he was now being isolated. There had been no strategic plan for improving the school in previous administrations, and Mrs G did not produce one either. He had not had the time, and he was not given the resources to produce such a plan. It was judged that he needed a strengthened senior leadership team and experienced subject leaders to support subject teachers.

As Easter approached, the LA worried about the 5 A*-Cs again. Mr N was told that strenuous efforts should be made with those Year 11 children most likely to achieve good GCSE passes. The authority would send in the teachers, fund off-site coaching classes and set up revision sessions. The school's staff did not approve. Mr N's view was that it made no difference. 'You are talking about kids who have not learnt for such a long time. Doing GCSE maths they did not have the background. They just did not know enough'. It was an example of another short-term fix, itself poorly implemented, which disregarded the fundamental and endemic problems. And it failed.

The Director convened a meeting of headteachers from Thanet and the wider area. He put to them that this was a school in their area which was failing the students and asked what they would do to help. He made it plain that all the headteachers had colluded in placing and sustaining The Ramsgate School in its present position. The idea he promoted was that a group of heads would support a colleague head who was in difficulty by 'loaning staff, sharing expertise and not "dumping" on the school'. Usually requests for support of this sort were for new, inexperienced, heads. Mr N began to talk to his union.

Several headteachers came to look round Ramsgate to see if they would take it on. And after an initial visit, Mr H, a Canterbury headteacher with a reputation for straight talking and toughness, then spent three days in the school. He talked to many people who were quite open with him and said what they thought should happen. He never talked to Mr N but he took soundings from teachers at all levels and talked to pupils, 'wandering around the back end of the playground, which is a good way to do it'. Then he went to the Director with the idea that, if this team of heads was not coming in, he was prepared to put a team together, largely from his own school, with the hope that Mr C, once at his school but now a deputy at another school, would join them.

Mr H drew up an action plan, which was to support the school's senior management for one year in establishing systems, getting the discipline right, modelling the behaviours, getting the teaching improved and the prospects for improved attainment in place. The Director approved the action plan, but it did not include Mr N. He was assured that he was still the head. He told staff and wrote to parents saying what a marvellous plan this was to help the school. Unsurprisingly, however, the transition to the new set of school leaders was even messier than in the earlier transitions. Clashes occurred from the outset as the arrangement proved unworkable. Within two weeks, Mr H and Mr N agreed that this rescue plan could not work with Mr N in place.

The Director had already visited with a personnel officer and Mr N talked further with his union. The view was that there was not a head in the county who would not accept the deal offered to him to go. By Mr N's reckoning, it cost the county £300,000 to get rid of him, eight years ahead of when he would have retired. He judged that, 'the Director might have felt I had been too slow – and maybe he was right'.

ENDNOTE

That ended Mr N's period as headteacher and he could look back to watch the urgent, vigorous and 'absolutely horrendous' approach subsequently adopted. 'That team ran riot', he said.

In more general terms, as Mr N saw it, 'It takes four years when you take charge of a grotty secondary modern and during that time you change admissions attracting more able children and more middle class parents.' All the time the school had been struggling, KCC support was often compromised and never sufficient. Mr K had suddenly been faced with a budget problem; almost as soon as she took up her post, Mrs G had to take a block of new pupils mid-year with no help. Meanwhile, a sense of being ground down and of just surviving was strong and growing amongst the ever-changing staff. Pupils had no belief in their school or themselves, and no faith that the school would do anything for them. The negatives about the school had become so public that it determined a downward spiral. The Minister at Westminster, the Leader of the Council, the cabinet member for education as well as the new Director were concerned at the fate of this school, which was again at the bottom of the league tables and, in 2003, judged to be 'failing'.

SCHOOL IMPROVEMENT AND BLOOD ON THE TRACKS

INTRODUCTION

It is intriguing to observe the escalation in efforts to solve the school's problems, which hitherto had been quite obviously inadequate, untargeted and with no clear strategic approach. Even the new team's remedies could not be regarded as thought through in any sophisticated way. This improvement initiative was not going to rely on the efforts of others and did not depend on attracting a different clientele. It certainly inflicted pain, damage, pace and uncompromising removal of poor teachers to try to raise educational standards and life chances for young people in the area.

Mr H led the team in having secured the absolute backing of the Director. The initial agreement covered one year in which to model senior management team (SMT) good practice. It became plain to the incoming team that this would not work, and to the sitting headteacher that this was an impossible relationship. From the summer half term of 2003, the team of Mr H and four colleagues were in charge. The whole project had been taken on at the centre of the LA, out of the hands of lesser groups. The Director was in control of The Ramsgate School improvement, with the District Schools Officer as the person on the ground through whom communications would be managed, action required by others would be agreed and resources would be requested. Under these conditions, Mr H could say, 'We never had any doubts that we would deliver'.

The total focus was demonstrable by their concentration on only the core business and internal priorities. No frivolities, distractions or loosely targeted enhancements from well-meaning outsiders were tolerated. One result of this was that, as a university researcher, I could not arrange a visit.

THE DIAGNOSIS

Mr H recognised that the school had been in a bad way for a very long time and had had a series of headteachers, 'who had made no difference whatsoever or, if anything, had just cemented the bad practice'. The Director thought it was a disgrace that there were schools like this in the county and that the politicians and officers at some levels were not the least bit interested in them. Mr H spoke in the most scathing terms about what he found at The Ramsgate School.

> I thought it was unbelievable. It was beyond anything that you could have imagined in a civilised, rich country with a proper education system. I had to ask a child on the stairs if this was break or lesson time, as I could not tell, and I was told it was lesson time. There were kids, adults and a building – that was

as near to being a school as it got. It was just horrendous. The kids were safer out on the estate than they were in the school and the estate was pretty dangerous. It could not have been got out of special measures in a year, it was just too bad. It was the worst place anywhere in the world I had ever been in. It was just so awful in every respect that you could think of. There was no element that you could say was better than awful. Most of the people who worked there worked there because they couldn't work anywhere else. …

Some of the TAs were very good and had the pupils' interests at heart but staff had the attitude that they could not be sacked because there were no others to take their place. That had been the reason why successive heads had got nowhere because they had believed the folklore. There were hardly any qualified staff but the view the heads had taken was that they had to work with what they had, "but they were crap, so I'll give up", and that is what every head had done. Some might have tried for a year, 18 months and then given up. These heads went in on their own. They did not have enough volume of competence to start to make a difference, whereas this time there was a team, four quality people, however they had been put together. They knew each other and I knew that if I asked them to do something they would do it and do it well, but were strong enough to tell me if they thought it was not the right thing to do.

That was the initial view and, as someone who had been there at the time, I could not disagree with it or the extreme way in which it was expressed.

THE TEAM AND THE PLAN

The make up of the team coming to The Ramsgate School, with further back up from Mr H's school in Canterbury, was decided more by accident than design. Mr H had to get governors at his school to agree first.

I had this magnificent team. I had a head of English (Mr M), an ex-head of maths (Ms N), another who was great with kids – old-fashioned discipline maybe (Mr K) – and a fourth who was brilliant with organisation and the detail (Mr C). A stunning team, …

They were capable of being a team straightaway in terms of their skills and complementary specialisms. All knew the way Mr H worked, the model of the school he ran and what the plan would be. They did not have to learn how to work together. One member of the team described how, before agreeing, he wanted to know the make up of the team. It had to be the right people who knew each other and trusted each other. He wanted to be sure that if 'something happened' he would know their reaction and that it would be a supportive one. He did not know the others well, just colleagues who did an excellent job, and so bought in. They had a saying, 'would you go over the top for them? .. take a bullet for them?' Loyalty was already established, and Mr H had total confidence in them and they in each other, but he had to win them over to come into the team. There had not been an LEA team equipped to do the job. Indeed, the Director suggested that another option was to put one of his senior staff in, but that did not prove possible at the time. The team for the rescue initiative was quite fortuitously available.

Whilst running The Ramsgate School, Mr H remained the headteacher of The Canterbury High School, itself a school in challenging circumstances and later a National Challenge school. It required the support of the Canterbury governors and the SMT for him to be seconded to run The Ramsgate School as well. Once in The Ramsgate School, Mr H had for the most part a 'political role': 'I dealt with everything external to the day to day running of the school, namely, DCSF, Ofsted, Kent LEA, the Academies Division, Thanet headteachers, Steve Ladyman (the local MP), the unions etc'. From the outset, Mr H decided that Mr C should be the de facto headteacher of The Ramsgate School in the eyes of the parents and students, conveying the absolute confidence he had in Mr C and giving a clear line of communication for children and parents. Mr H suspected that the parents and children would not have known of his existence; this was true of parents and children I interviewed. As the legal headteacher, Mr H did, in addition, retain a veto on all decisions, but his only involvement in the direct running of the school was in dealing with staff, some appointments, all disciplinary and competence procedures and being available to offer advice and support to the team.

This arrangement also brought a supportive relationship with The Canterbury High School staff, in some cases through pairing of staff, mainly clerical and technical, and individual teachers coming to The Ramsgate School to teach on some programmes and to run after-school course work sessions in a range of subjects

Asked whether there was a plan, Mr H said, 'No. Well, yes. It was to support the senior management, but there was none.' Even without a plan, the determination at the highest level was that this school would be changed, that behaviour would improve and that results would rise. But everything started from a very low level. The school was talked about venomously by parents. Staff were exceedingly negative and a view accepted by many was that it would only get worse (but quickly) before it got better.

The four members of the new team were upgraded, and therefore received increased salaries, but there was no increase for Mr H initially; retrospectively, he received £10,000 for each year. It was just something, he said, that had to be done, 'a mission'. In his view, the task was simple: 'Making a bad school OK is not complicated, though it is hard work. You have only got to do two things: you've got to get kids to behave and then you've got to teach them something.' Mr C as the substantive headteacher was signed up to this simple perspective as were the other team members.

THE TREATMENT

The team returned after the summer half term holiday to take control and 'hit the place between the eyes', as Mr H put it in his characteristic combative style. A KCC education officer said, 'They went in like a SWAT team'.

What happened was instant and dramatic. The first part of the solution was, 'to take on the children and their bad behaviour. We knew we had to win and we thought it would take until Christmas, but in fact we had it cracked by the end of the summer term. Because it was so bad, they were desperate for improvement. The pupils, bar five per cent, actually wanted order, adults who set boundaries and cared about what they learned. Improving behaviour was setting down the rules, being really hard, really strict, consistent and following through.' One of the team gave his view:

> It was not that the school was out of control. The kids coming in were not off the wall, just demotivated. I saw pupils disillusioned in lessons where they did not try because work would not be marked and, in all likelihood, the same teacher would not be in front of them next week. Even a bright kid would say, 'There's no point,' and you had sympathy with his view. He had sussed it. It was a massive urban myth that the school was violent and aggressive.

At the same time they told the teaching staff that 'unless you can prove your competence, we will sack you'. Disciplinary procedures were promptly begun in the June and July period with 27 out of 34 staff. Twenty five left. No one was sacked. As they said, they went by the book and had the KCC personnel person in support which worked well. All of these staff were observed and had feedback, were observed again, were given some support, had targets set and then the judgement was given. It was unusually harsh and urgent. The staff had been told in an early staff meeting that 'the staff do not matter. We are here for the children'.

All the existing senior management team had difficulties with the new team, except one who – a departing teacher said – acted as, 'the liaison person between this foul management team and the body of the staff. And the staff loved her.' One of the deputies, originally part of the KCC School Support Team, was soon amongst those under disciplinary procedures; he moved elsewhere.

The team members were unshakeable in their support for the draconian steps, '100% behind it', as one said while another put it quite plainly: 'You had to ask, "would you want your child taught by that member of staff?", and if the answer is no, then they have to go'.

Though the team's job was hard, Mr H recounted a rule they had for themselves which was that you had to arrive in the school with a smile on your face and sometimes the managers had to sit in their cars and compose themselves for that. It was important not to give any sign to staff or pupils that you were worried or frightened. This show of confidence had to be maintained all day. Then they would gather in one of the offices at the end of the day and debrief. It was to give the message that all was OK and they were in control though they owned that it was, for long periods, a façade.

Mr H, on Southern Television news, explained that staff were not up to the job and had to go. He said, 'I don't blame the staff. I blame the previous headteachers and the local authority that did not address the problems'. They ended the summer term of 2003 with 4% of pupils gaining five A* to C grades, the same as for the year before. The fast track dismissal system had worked and the unions, Mr H said, had been on the whole fairly reasonable. They had declared a dispute, but this may have been as much to persuade KCC to 'look after' those teachers moved on. There were exchanges at the very highest levels in KCC, which defused the tensions.

The school was then left with too few staff at the start of the Autumn term, 2003, and the leadership group asked the education authority, in effect the Director, if they could run the school for three days a week, but were told no. As a next best offer from the county, the Specialist Teacher Service were put in touch and they came out to meet with Mr H and Mr C. They were judged to have too little to offer.

Then the team set about recruiting. Having to keep the school open for five days a week and putting in huge effort to bring in teachers stretched their resources. They tried agencies unsuccessfully, and then went to Dublin airport to interview candidates, set up by an organisation there. They became knowledgeable about time zones and interviewing people by telephone all over the world at all times of the day and night English time. It was described as a mad four or five week period, with a spreadsheet showing the subjects for which they required replacements. KCC agreed to underwrite the rent for a property for the people to stay in on arrival – another attraction for people arriving from overseas who are to start teaching straightaway.

By January, they had 'restaffed the school with ... a United Nations of a teaching force', although some continuing staff said they were no improvement on those that had been 'persuaded' to leave. Indeed, this body of staff turned out to give no more than short term respite and it would have been clear quickly that this was not a permanent solution. 'It was the beginning of another dark chapter'. They could open the school for five days a week but it was a culture shock for this in-coming group. A number, recruited in Ireland, lasted a few days, and two stayed for around two terms. As the year wore on, The Ramsgate School was able to recruit teachers from England, who were familiar with the national curriculum and courses in English secondary schools, and was able to pay extra allowances to attract such staff.

However, these were still Ramsgate School children, many of whom had not got into the required scholarly habits. Some exhibited very challenging behaviour, others were very needy, and teachers had to be highly skilled.

Though many replacements were unsatisfactory, it bought time and allowed the team to work on the Year 11s to get a tripling of the 5A*-C grades in the summer of 2004, which gave the school, its leadership and plans some credibility. It would, they felt, get them the staff they required and improve all round confidence for the second full year.

As Mr C put it, 'Kent helped us get rid of the staff but there was no end plan. A lot of our thinking and action was quite linear'. Asked to draw up a list of people 'who cannot teach properly' they did that and 'moved them on'. Clearly there was no master plan, only a series of necessary steps even though they knew there was potential chaos in view. The team was fire-fighting, as the managers put it, even if some of these fires were of their own lighting, picking off every issue as it arose. Only later did they feel they had bought themselves leadership time and could bring things under control. In the first year, the senior managers spent a lot of time not in their offices but out in the corridors and visiting classes. They were also role modelling and doing things that some of the staff had never seen before – smiling, talking cheerfully to young people.

All five of the team had to be patrolling the school and actually teaching. The team struggled on using whatever staff they could get but none came from other Thanet schools. Youth workers and classroom assistants helped the team and sometimes there were 100 children in the hall and one person supervising.

INSPECTORS AND MONITORING

HMI were clearly strong allies amongst the few that the leadership group had. All the way through the series of monitoring visits the HMI reports contained positive phrases about the energy, determination, single-mindedness of the team in putting the pupils' needs first. In the first year HMI commented critically on, 'a lack of an overarching LEA strategy' for paving the way towards the intended academy, mirrored by the leadership team's own admission of having a serial approach to tackling problems. The loss of 25 teachers and the unsatisfactory replacements from anywhere in the world led to a 'dislocation', as the HMI put it, before further staff could be recruited, particularly to middle management or head of department positions.

The second monitoring visit in November 2003 reported the following:

> The executive headteacher and the seconded leadership team have taken determined and radical action to address the high proportion of unsatisfactory and ineffective teaching, recognising that too many of the existing staff did not have the capacity or the expertise to make the improvements that were urgently needed. Working with significant support from the LEA personnel team, over half the teaching staff were placed on competency procedures. A comprehensive package of development, support and monitoring was implemented, with additional resources provided by the LEA. The outcome of these actions has been the departure of almost half the teachers, resulting in significant gaps in staffing in the short term.

HMI hoped that the start of the new term in January 2004 would see a radically improved climate and accelerating progress though it was 'too early to assess the impact of the decisive action that has been taken.' The inspectors acknowledged the seriousness of the school's situation, which 'demanded vigorous action', and the response of the senior managers as being 'brave and clear sighted.'

Though attendance had improved to 83.5%, it was judged to be very low – in lessons observed attendance was only 75% – and punctuality both to school and to lessons was unsatisfactory. The school's roll was falling because pupils left, but Mr H and Mr C strove to restrict casual entries and excluded many. The educational task was still huge.

In March 2004, the third monitoring inspection took place one year into the management regime of the new team, and reported: 'the school has made *limited progress* since the last monitoring inspection and limited progress overall since being subject to special measures.' This was a very damaging judgement. The HMI report identified the clash between the LEA's programme of support and the school managers' focus on pupils' learning. The inspectors backed the school managers' judgment,' and noted the breakdown of trust and confidence between the school and the authority.

Although new staff had arrived, this had presented a huge induction challenge. The new staff with overseas qualifications had been given additional time away from teaching, and the LEA had proposed a comprehensive programme of support for them, but this had not had a positive impact on improving the quality of teaching. Teaching was satisfactory or better in less than half of the 28 lessons observed, 'a marked decline'. Many of the weak lessons 'started late and failed to engage the pupils... expectations too low.... unable to control pupils... too many lessons simply petered out.' There is nonetheless praise for the leadership group which has 'continued to work tirelessly to maintain morale and support the new teachers.' They note a modest improvement in pupils' behaviour, with pupils subject to exclusion having fallen from 20% last year to about 15% so far this year, but 'attendance remains low and punctuality remains severely problematic', and in lessons, 'the attitudes and behaviour were at least satisfactory in only half the lessons … a considerable deterioration' … to a level worse than that reported in January 2003, when the school was put in special measures in Mr N's short time as headteacher. One year into the team's presence in the school, inspectors reported that 'too many staff have adopted an approach of undue tolerance that frequently gives pupils the upper hand, with pupils at times taking over lessons and exercising power without responsibility'. This could have been a time when the team gave up or the local authority lost faith. One can imagine the smirks of those who had left when under the competency assessments.

Just as Mr H had been fierce about his condemnation of the state of The Ramsgate School at the outset of their work, so now he turned to the LEA with a blistering three page letter. In early April 2004, he wrote a letter to the Director which was nothing short of explosive and hugely worrying, especially when they were a year into their work turning the school around. Mr H said his letter was a blunt and honest view with no vindictiveness but was just about addressing the issues for the benefit of the children of The Ramsgate School. It began by stating that at the last HMI visit the school failed every key indicator and quite radically suggested that one solution was to withdraw from the LEA and operate independently.

This was most definitely the exercise of Mr H's political role. His message was threefold: the LEA had not helped enough, indeed had got in the way; the poor report from Ofsted was more the fault of the LEA for not delivering its backing sufficiently; and the near future should involve the sort of backing Mr H required.

He acknowledged five elements that worked:

one specialist teacher; youth service – they enabled us to keep the school open; evidence gathering for competence procedures until [named person] changed sides; bits of personnel; budget support.

He gave a list of the things required.

– ASTs (Advanced Skills Teachers) who teach (not ones who pontificate)
– Specialist Teachers –'as many as possible to teach literacy to children'
– Personnel to sort out longstanding issues; too many staff have taken the LEA for a ride for years
– support for two development days on behaviour management/ assertiveness: if the LEA genuinely has someone who could lead, we'd be grateful. Otherwise we will do it ourselves.

The third part, under the heading, 'What has gone wrong?', was followed by an absolute onslaught, the like of which is seldom found in professional files.

– The LEA does not listen… adds to our workload
– Formal complaint about a KCC officer who withdrew an AST shortly before HMI visit
– ASTs were to be seconded in from other schools but this has not happened
– A senior officer promising 20 teachers from the Specialist Team (only one appeared) that is why they had to go to Dublin and appoint teachers from the four corners of the globe and this has caused all sorts of problems including failing the HMI visit
– The odd specialist teacher who turns up, arrives at 10 and leaves after lunch.
– There is an accusation of bullying of Mr C by two [named] senior officers.
– It is as if LEA officers are too scared to do anything or, and possibly more likely, do not believe that anything will change at Ramsgate. Where is the sharing of good practice in an LEA that has more failing schools than any other?
– LEA teams are not self managing – it takes hours of our time to manage them.
– LEA advisers have no accountability … they waltz in and out with no achieved outcomes
– LEA advisors get embroiled in staff problems. I have refused to have some back on site!
– The KS 3 strategy team failed to follow requests; their behaviour was appalling. That is why two of them were banned from the school.
– The school was twice directed to take very difficult students and was deceived as to their characteristics.

This all has to be read in the context of a continuing and unwavering support from the Director, and Mr H's unshaken faith in three of the KCC senior staff involved.

The letter concluded with mockery at the allocation of an officer to carry out weekly reviews of their work in the school. The way forward was stated as to distance themselves from the 'so-called' school improvement branch of the LEA. 'We will do more for the children by acting alone than we will in "partnership" with you. You do not need to know our plans for the future – you have no role to play in them'.

While this might have been 'over the top', as some recipients saw it, the purpose was served. The letter both deflected blame and gained a promise of resources. It was a marker that Mr H's team would not be the victims in this battle, and not judged as failing as others had been in this most difficult of schools. As one of the team said, 'Mr H's role was fantastic; he kept people at bay, fought our corner and dealt with all the politics'. The broader context for KCC was concern about another twelve schools which were seriously underperforming, and reform of the county's advisory service to deal with these problems.

After Easter 2004, two of the team taught all the Year 11s in the hall together with some guest presenters coming in to contribute. One described it as a desperate remedy. They did exam preparation, test papers, revision activities. 'We thought attendance would go down, but it went up. The kids thought someone cared, was trying and they were learning something'.

The Ramsgate School ended the summer term 2004 with 15% 5A*-C passes, the best ever on record. This had been achieved through very swift and radical strategies, partly prompted by the *limited progress* judgement. Because there were so few qualified teachers, they were assigned new classroom roles. They made classes huge, maybe 50 children and only used the largest rooms. They would have a lead teacher whose job was to plan and deliver outstanding learning for those children. That teacher would be supported, extraordinarily, by three others, sometimes more. Each class had a class coach who would go round with them and whose job it was to know the children very well. If any pupil 'kicked off', they would manage that pupil's behaviour. There would be two other teachers whose job was to support the learning and teaching that was going on, to do all the marking and to feed back to the lead teacher on the learning that the pupils had covered. All the lead teachers were very good.

The vocational learning and BTEC courses were a curriculum change crucial to the improvement in 5A*-Cs. Complementing this was 'the strategy of identifying students with the potential to get 5A*-Cs and coaching them in the subjects where they had the likelihood of getting a grade. The trouble was that the others who did not have that potential were discarded. They also brought in coursework coaches, because that is the one thing the teacher has absolute control over in the GCSE; if you get the highest possible coursework grade then you are going to get a high grade overall.'

A small number of teachers came over from The Canterbury High School to teach, two on a weekly basis. One reported her surprise at the lack of structure and routines but found the students responsive to organised and well-resourced teaching. Again, because it was going to be demanding on students, they expected attendance to be poor, but it was not.

The team had difficulties with a whole range of agencies. In a later interview, Mr H reported that working with the county advisory service had proved to be difficult, 'because they did not want to play my game'. Mr H found them wanting to be supportive and pleasant to staff to the detriment of the pupils. They sided so strongly with the staff that it did not help with the urgent need to improve teaching. Mr C found them counterproductive. Mr H, as executive head, simply stopped them coming to the school, 'It was not that they were getting in the way; they were a positive nightmare.'

On exclusions they felt they did not get much support from the local authority. The local exclusions officer contested things though they thought the Director would probably have backed them. One can calculate the problem that arises when the school which has been a receiver of excluded children – and largely keeps them – becomes an excluder and it is difficult to find places for the pupils to go to in the local area. The lack of support from other local secondary schools was said to have greatly disappointed the Director who had been encouraging collaboration since his arrival in the county. Within two years he had succeeded in reorganising the LA's schools into partnership structures. It became common for schools to collaborate and share staff, and a unified headteacher group was set up.

The school governors were reportedly difficult. 'The governors were an absolute, complete and utter nightmare … stand-up rows with governors.' They lost the powers to run the school – especially over personnel and finance. He reminded them that the team was in the school because of the state of the school that they had allowed to develop.

There was also pressure from the DCSF Academies Division who wanted evidence of progress in this school which was expected to come into the academies fold. The academies initiative to solve the problem of England's failing schools was high stakes political business with much happening behind the scenes. The Ramsgate School team also had strained relations with the appointed principal of the Academy. He took up his post one year before the opening of the Academy and was accommodated in a primary school on the estate.

Even at this time and with these interim consequences, there was no criticism from the county's most senior officers or from HMI about the drastic staff clear-out, the means by which it was done, or other steps taken from exclusion to refusing to take new pupils. It was accepted as 'the only show in town', a final extreme effort that had to go way beyond anything that had been tried and resourced before. The later HMI monitoring visit reports offered the judgment that progress has been 'reasonable' until January 2005 when it was 'good'. Mr H felt the school could have come out of special measures then, but the HMI team wanted the decision left to the original HMI team leader who had taken such an interest in the school.

The report which brought the school out of special measures in March 2005 stated, 'The school has improved rapidly during the last year and now provides a satisfactory education for its pupils'. At this successful endpoint, the school was judged to have 'a positive ethos and a settled climate for learning and was awarded the Investors in People Standard, meeting the requirements at a high level'. Pupils' behaviour was sound and the teaching satisfactory or better in all 24 lessons. Attendance was up to 86% and there was no mention of children arriving late to school, late to lessons and wandering around the building. The pupils' learning was at last matching the quality of teaching. Again there was praise for the leadership team, 'determined ... radical steps ... prepared to rethink their approach when progress stalls'.

The relatively high level of financial support was clearly a boon and this included the seconding in of staff for particular positions. Five of these were Advanced Skills Teachers and it made up for the lack of staff support from the other secondary schools in Thanet. The GCSE outcome for the summer of 2005 was 18%.

STAFF COMPETENCE AND THREATS OF DISMISSAL

Those staff members on the receiving end of this treatment were understandably mostly negative, at best joking about Mr H's team being the Gestapo, and using terms like vicious, brutal, aggressive, bastards, bullying, boot camp, long knives and 'the Italian Job' (alluding to Mr C's heritage). A number admitted that there was some justice in the approach and some appalling practice had to be eradicated. One said that, 'It was absolutely not the way to turn a school around', though admitting that the team's commitment was total and they set a standard for hard work and long hours that had been missing. It was acknowledged that Mr H 'wanted desperately for the school to be better for the children. He was there for the children'. One teacher recalls the first half term of the team's control in 2003 as 'horrendous, quite unprofessional in many ways. Staff were shouted at, told they were rubbish, that they were all incompetent.' The mixed responses from staff could be contained within a single sentence: 'They were bastards, but the kids loved Mr C'.

At the mention that their reign was described in very negative terms – like Gestapo – Mr H said 'Gestapo, they lost didn't they? We won. We were better than them. If we had been the Gestapo, you'd all be speaking German now'. He went on to say that this also demonstrated the humour they had which was important in keeping them going.

Mr H felt, on later reflection, that what they did wrong was not doing anything about the curriculum soon enough. Had he realised the error, the team would have made the necessary changes and, he thought, obtained double the number of 5A*-Cs in the second year because the pupils would have sat more vocational and practical subjects. The associated content and style of learning was so much more suitable for the children, and there was a member of staff who was experienced in the development of such courses. He felt that later changes helped the new academy meet its targets since it had a suitable curriculum to work with, and it enabled the school to meet its DCSF targets.

There were a number of myths about The Ramsgate School which the team identified. The team were told there was no point in having a public event for parents because they would not come or they would heckle. They challenged this, because they thought the children needed to see their achievements celebrated, whatever they were, and at the end of their first summer term, they had an event and the hall was packed. It was another bit of folklore proved wrong.

It was another myth that parents did not care. As Mr C said, 'We were excluding pupils by the dozen and they soon showed they cared, 'even if they sometimes expressed it in ways which were not easy to deal with'. But beneath it all you could see they did care and would come in very quickly when their child was given a two-day exclusion. They coped with these parents' upsets and it was important that the team met that challenge. They took the view, 'We will meet the parents wherever they are. If the parent is there, aggressive and shouting, we'll meet the parent there. We won't do the middle-class, high-falutin' thing. It was coming down to their level and was very robust', explaining that if their child continues to behave like that, it would lead to a permanent exclusion. Parents by year two were good and they were able to invite people in. As one parent said admiringly, 'That Mr C, you knew where you were with him. You knew he was in charge'.

Exclusions from The Ramsgate School had been high since 1996. The proportion of permanent exclusions from The Ramsgate was always around a quarter of all permanent exclusions in Thanet, when the school had only about 7% of the Thanet school population. Fixed period exclusions from the school accounted for one third of the total from Thanet secondary schools for much of this period. With 11 permanent exclusions in 2002/03, it was 26% of Thanet's total. This rose to 27 individuals in the first full year of the new team's reign, 43% of the total, and 36% of the Thanet's fixed period exclusions. In fact, the percentage of Thanet's children at The Ramsgate School had dropped below 7% as pupils were put out and the shutters were down, as far as possible, against the admission of new children during the year.

Mr H refused to take pupils from other schools and tried very hard to hold that line, even to the extent of the DCSF paying a visit and saying that because the school had spaces they had to take them. They took in only a few. They also had help from the future sponsor of the academy in setting up an off-site unit for some of these pupils.

The school was also at the receiving end of every and any initiative which came into the county. The benevolent view taken was that The Ramsgate School would benefit from all these inputs. In fact, they disrupted the school's working and were not the school's priorities. So these too were limited and judiciously selected.

The team of five saw themselves as holding the place together and though there were some others who could be given jobs, 'there was no one else you could rely on for the big stuff'. The team grew slightly as others who could be trusted were identified and invited to join them. One of those described how he was approached with an invitation, 'You seem to be one of the few people the kids listen to. We want you to join our management team.' He enjoyed this period, was impressed by the commitment and respected the fact that the new management were reasonable with him and did not insist that he go in and assess former colleagues.

The team refused to blame the children, the parents or the estates. Whilst acknowledging deprivation, it was not a big concern. They judged that the neighbourhood may have been more deprived than the other estates they had worked on but regarded this not as a reason to lower standards or expectations but all the more reason to raise standards, believing it to be the way out for young people if they could be successful in school.

In the final year of their period in control, the school was reportedly much calmer. The transformation was a contrast. They had installed play equipment, giant Lego type material, table tennis. Mr H reported finding his senior staff in the summer of 2005 actually sitting out in the playground at a break-time sunning themselves, maybe just an additional demonstration of their ability to now relax with the children and enjoy them. More telling was a lunch time visit from the District Schools Officer, who, walking around said that something was different, but she could not put her finger on it until she suddenly exclaimed, 'The children are playing. I have never seen the children playing before'. It was apparently safe for children to be children and that comment meant a great deal to the team.

EXIT FROM THE RAMSGATE SCHOOL

The team found it difficult when the transfer was imminent. Everything for them ended on the last day of term in July 2005. There was elation at getting out of special measures in March and later at the results. It was the end of the journey. 'It was a job well done and we did not need anyone to tell us'. The Director came at the last day to convey his thanks. They recorded that they had no complaints with the Director at any point and his support had been unwavering. Mr H returned full time to The Canterbury High School and other team members were eventually found other positions. One got a retirement package. There is no disguising that it was a difficult period with knowledge of the approaching hand over to the Academy principal and that, after all their work, none of the team would be part of the new order. One concern was that, if the success of the Marlowe Academy resulted in the creation of a new Ramsgate style 'sink' school somewhere else, the end result would be a failure, merely passing the poisoned chalice around.

Mr J, the incoming Academy principal, was generous on public occasions about the work done by the team in preparing the school for academy status. The team met at another school to look at the results which had risen to 18% achieving 5 A*-C GCSEs in the summer of 2005 and could congratulate themselves on another rise. The 'lift-off' is evident in Figure 6.1, although there is some way to go to approach the ever-rising national percentage. Visually it does demonstrate the years of rock bottom performance from which they departed.

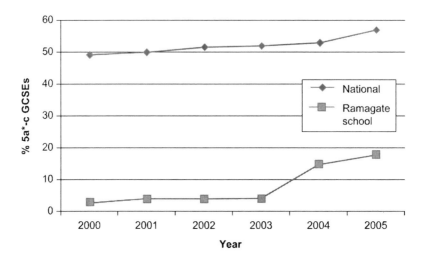

Figure 6.1. GCSE results at The Ramsgate School and nationally 2000–2005.

They had certainly been resolute, unbending, focussed and determined, never doubting that they would succeed. Mr H said,

> We made a lot of enemies. We made enemies with everybody that worked in Kent … we upset personnel, the advisory service because we had basically kicked them out … we upset the DCSF, everybody … by doing the right thing, just not letting go, refusing to compromise.

They retained the support of the three senior officers, including the Director, who acknowledged the extremity of the challenge, the ruthlessness (he preferred 'robustness') needed, and the urgency that had never been exercised before. HMI also provided a constant and unwavering support. The lead HMI introduced herself at the first monitoring visit saying, 'It is my job to help you get this school out of special measures', and this is what she clearly did.

The Director of Education said that the team, in their two years, had stabilised the school with the 'brute sanity' that was needed. Without their work, the transition to an academy would have been difficult. Everything else had been tried, and he said of Mr H:

> If there was a robust form of management it was for the children. The place had not existed for the children before. Mr H said to the staff when he came in that this is not a school that exists for you; it exists for the children and this is what we are going to do for them. He did get my backing and would again. There are not many people who would step up to do this. He has a bravery and he has a track record of doing things and he worked tirelessly to achieve things.

One of the team referred to it as, 'The best two and a half years of my teaching career', and another as, 'The hardest job I have ever done, but one of the most satisfying'. Mr H reflected on the enormity of the challenge with typical black humour and judged that it had reduced his life expectancy.

ENDNOTE

This school was not a bad school because of radical ideological commitments[12] to pupil freedom, curriculum absurdities or malevolent professional practices. In under-resourced, challenging circumstances there can be a battering of staff morale, a shattering of previously secure expertise and a downward spiral of expectation and aspiration. At The Ramsgate School, there even appeared to be a breakdown in notions of plain human respect for the children and families for whom the school existed.

There are limits to the levels of ruthlessness, or robustness, which 'professionals' will usually apply. There are also limits to which overarching bodies like local authorities are willing to get their hands dirty with urgent changes that push at the boundaries of legality. But more than that, such changes are hugely damaging to the professionals who may themselves have had poor support and were trying, if failing, to do a good job in dispiriting circumstances.

The Ramsgate School had between 450 and 600 pupils during the period when they were given an appalling education, miseducation even, as the habits they were acquiring and the attitudes that were being reinforced were often negative and anti-social. Added to this, the skills with which they left the school would be quite inadequate in what was already a highly competitive local employment market. Some professionals might talk fatalistically about three generations of worklessness in a family (if you can find one) and see little that the school can contribute to the future of children coming from that family. On the other side, if the pupils are to come first, one can understand a policy of resolute personnel management towards those not seen as up to the job, not delivering, and behaving in ways which protected them but failed children.

In thinking about *blame*, which I return to in Chapter 11, one must recognise the great harm done to pupils who are not properly taught, in schools that are not adequately staffed, in areas where the levels and range of unmet need are high. The damage to huge numbers of children is immense, and lasts lifetimes. Between 1996 and 2003, almost 600 pupils from the area would have left the school at 16. Not only were their results derisory, but their prospects of employment were poor. We can blame the state for the levels of poverty, the education authority for the tardy arrival of resources and a lack of determination to correct things, and the big myth of 'professionalism' which is so often about collective self-protection to the detriment of the client group of children and families. The 'unprofessional' way in which Mr H's 'hit team' set about the improvement task with urgency, merely swept away the myth of it being preferable for people to turn up to do the job badly while deserving sympathy for the difficulties their work involved. Some staff left because they could not see the school improving. Some stayed because to leave would have been to admit it would not improve, though that often left the guilt feeling of collusion in a routinely and repetitively failing arrangement.

This fierce, merciless approach to school improvement is not visible in the academic literature.[13] Some might say that making the necessary changes could have been done differently. However, two considerations should be borne in mind. Much had been tried before; and even this approach faltered badly at one point through lack of staff and the poor quality of newly recruited staff. It was very much about zero tolerance of poor teaching and speed in executing the change. Despite Mr H's mid-term onslaught on the LEA, there were senior officers who were supportive and respected and who did funnel resources to the school. There was political support from KCC, national government and HMI who backed the team's judgement through all the ups and downs over the two years. It did require determination on the ground in the school with a focus on how those actually working there could collectively make a difference.

The Academy opened just when The Ramsgate School achieved its best ever examination results in the summer of 2005 having emerged from special measures earlier the same year. Going to the last Ramsgate School jamboree before it closed in August 2005, the Director spoke warmly of, 'The difference in the way the staff came together, the sense of knowing what young people were capable of was palpable and so, so different from what had gone before'.

THE ACADEMY – VISION, PRINCIPLES, STRUCTURES AND ETHOS OF A NEW BEGINNING

THE PHOENIX SYNDROME

No new beginning is ever new. Certainly, in September 2005, the name was new, a lot of the teachers were new – but just under half of the original staff transferred (TUPEd)[14] to the Academy from The Ramsgate School. It was the same building to begin with, but for a few modifications, and the pupils were largely the same, though there was a new Year 7 and the old Year 11s had gone. The new Academy building opened one year into the Academy's life, looked across to the same Newington estate and the pupil ability on entry remained unchanged from years earlier. The Academy was meant to be as dramatic a change as could be created, fulfilling the vision of the Director of Education, KCC's leading politicians, Roger De Haan, the philanthropic sponsor, and Mr J when he was appointed as Principal.

The Academy plan was very much driven by the new Director. The initial steps to the opening of the Academy began in 2002 and required changes in government policy which the then Minister for Education, Charles Clark, was persuaded to make after lobbying by the Director and leader of the council. This allowed academies to be established outside cities in what was until then the *City Academies* Scheme. Kent, by some counts the largest education authority in the country, was a significant player on the national political stage and could expect to be listened to by national government. The Marlowe was Kent's first academy and the first non-city academy, the big solution to the increasingly high profile failing school. The leader of the council, referred to as 'a true one nation Tory, a believer in equality of opportunity', was very keen to address the Kent ultra-failing school problem. This was to be done without dismantling the selective system whereby 30% of the county's ablest children were creamed off to grammar schools. Collectively, local politicians had made it clear that improving the lowest performing schools was now a priority, and one which exercised national politicians up to ministerial level.

The first full academy proposal was drafted in April, 2002 for what was initially named the 'Ramsgate Academy'.[15] Mrs G, who left in the summer of 2002 enjoyed her contribution to drafting the application. The project held every prospect of being hugely radical and, at a low point towards the end of her tenure at The Ramsgate School, a solution to all the challenges she could not overcome.

This application for Kent's first academy was somewhat fraught. They had to find sponsorship and the deadline for the current phase of applications was imminent. At a Partnership Board meeting, someone said to the Director, 'You look glum', to which he replied that he had just been to The Ramsgate School again, 'And all I need is someone to give me a million pounds.' Mr De Haan, then Chief Executive of Saga, quietly said he would help out and his million was formally offered in a letter of June 2002. The leader of the council wrote in the same month to the education minister to report Mr De Haan's commitment and, while still hopeful that one of the other charities or grant schemes would match this, the county would pledge the other £1M so as not to delay plans. This was an innovative financial solution, retained a LA stake in the school and meant that it could be seen as part of the community of schools serving an area. Representing how this had all come about as quite fortuitous, the Director said, 'The right people came together at the right time'. In March 2004, the Secretary of State agreed to enter a formal funding agreement for the Academy, which meant funding approaching £30M would become available.

The Director was clear that The Ramsgate School needed root and branch change. He had seen the tail-end of one improvement attempt, the short stay of another head and had backed the 'robust' two year team school improvement effort from 2003 to 2005. The strategy has to be understood in the context of Kent's schools in the so-called Club 25 – those not achieving 25% A*-C GCSEs on a regular basis, at one point numbering 30.

THE BUILDING

The Academy building was stunning both from the exterior and from inside where you are greeted by an arched atrium area with an open-out theatre space on one side and walkways stretching up three floors on the other. The architects were BDP (Building, Design Partnership), a major international practice of architects, designers, engineers and urbanists. Their brief for The Marlowe was to:

– create an inspirational learning environment for 1200 students
– open up school facilities to the local community
– break free from conventional ideas about school design

The architects saw it as 'an inspiring secondary school for the 21st century .... a whole student town under a single roof with the UK's longest spanning Kerto grid shell[16] in a landscaped arena that draws the local public in to share the facilities'.

As the Director said of the building, shown in Figure 7.1, 'It smacks you in the face visually. It was to say to the community, "This is the best we can give you and you deserve it. Now use it!"' It was planned as an 11–18 school for 1,200 pupils, where previously it was 11–16 with only very small numbers continuing to some Year 12 courses.

Figure 7.1. The Marlowe Academy 2006.

By 2011, Kent had ten academies, all funded on a similar partnership basis with KCC. Roger De Haan was a business partner in four.

THE ACADEMY PLAN AND THE NATIONAL PICTURE

From the Director's wide experience, he could see that, with over 1,000 secondary schools (out of 4,500 in England) having less than 30% 5A*-C GCSEs, it was obvious how to improve some of them quite quickly: 'You deal with the quality of teaching and learning, you improve the quality and use of data for better targeting, better support for homework, better ICT, better management, and these would all be relatively simple things to do'. For the 300 or 400 schools left, the tougher challenges, a community renewal strategy was needed and academies could contribute to that. He felt that some of those national challenge schools might well have been doing a much better job for the bottom 30% than was being done for the bottom 30% in higher performing comprehensives.

He explained that many comprehensive schools in England were bouncing along on 45 or 50% 5A*-Cs passes and there was no incentive for the head, governors or staff to invest in that bottom 30%, because they did not contribute much to the critical measure by which a school is judged, namely 5A*-Cs. Most schools can ignore their bottom 30% and get by. Sink schools, and The Ramsgate was unhelpfully labelled as foremost amongst them, were ALL bottom 30%. All the usual strategies were not an answer for The Ramsgate, because what it needed was this community renewal. 'It needed that engagement, that belief that for people who have been unemployed for god knows how long that they can have something better for their children. If you get it right, the academy offers the opportunity to go beyond parents' long term unemployment, generations of poverty, etc'.

As the Director said of taking the academy route, 'Creating a group of schools outside local authority control as a solution might sound daft but it wasn't. In an authority with 100-plus secondary schools, you can risk having 10, 15 academies. It can challenge the orthodoxy and assumptions about what you can do with deprived communities – and also act as a stimulus and challenge to other schools nearby. KCC is a partnership body for all of the academies and it is saying that, OK, Kent is a mixed economy of schools. We were putting in neighbourhood comprehensives, which is what academies were, into neighbourhoods of massive deprivation. It was a deliberate tactic.'

Both the leader of the council and the lead cabinet member for education were clear that they had to do something about this community and backed both the intervention approach (2003–05), led by Mr H, and the academy plan. They, too, could relate the malfunctioning of a long term failing school to neglected communities, greater numbers going into the criminal justice system, more teenage pregnancies and more unemployment.

THE TRANSITION TO BEING AN ACADEMY

The first headteacher of the Academy was Mr J, son of a country clergyman, who had been recruited from Oxfordshire, where he had a reputation as a head who could turn around a challenging school. From September 2004 he had the luxury of planning the new academy contributing to the design of the building and working on staffing and staff structures, and the curriculum, including the length of the school day.

At his previous school, he had made a huge impact and was highly regarded. The Director, previously Director of Education in Oxfordshire, had been impressed that, whenever there was trouble in his school, Mr J was in the thick of it, sorting it out. He came with a great track record, a 'hands–on person, omni-present in his school'. The Director knew he was academically very able and totally committed, with a true sense of direction. He understood why adolescents misbehaved, how you put it right, was balanced in his approach to staff management and had the right blend of skills and personality. He came with a group of people he knew and trusted and that was 'important when you have to hit the floor running'.

In the year prior to the academy opening, there was a 'creative tension', as some might kindly put it, between Mr J and the senior staff of The Ramsgate School, most notably with Mr H and Mr C. Mr J was based in a local primary school and not especially welcomed into The Ramsgate School which was dealing with its challenges, as detailed in Chapter 5. He was able to get to know the pupils and the community and it gave him time to get the ICT sorted and the curriculum modelled and presented to the trustees and DCSF.

In 2004, leaving The Ramsgate School in a fairly dispirited mood, the Director recalled talking to two of the pupils outside and asked, 'What do you think of your new school?' They said they had not really thought about it. He took them inside to the show them the model of the Academy building that would be in place in 2006 and told them, 'We are going to spend £30M on this and their response was, "Where are we going to go then?"' It just showed that the young people thought that nobody cared about them, they never got the good things, it always went somewhere else. It was still going to take a while to embed the change and develop aspirations, 'almost a generational thing'.

THE INSPIRATION

The ideas for The Marlowe Academy were drafted by Mr J on journeys between Oxford and London when travelling to the DCSF while he was still head of the school in Oxford. Maybe it was put flippantly as 'a blinding flash of inspiration in the back of a coach', but that is part of the apparently amiable and convivial style of this seasoned school leader.

Mr J's vision for the organisational style of the Academy was firmly fixed in his mind before he started in September 2005. This had been clearly influenced by his experiences in the school he turned around in Oxford: working with students, being accessible and visible, but also tailoring provision to local circumstances and to immediate challenges. While there were no gurus that Mr J followed, he had also drawn on his Education MA, and his middle management experience under the previous heads he had worked for. For The Marlowe, 'it was my design and it drew on everything else from my career and education previously', though from his previous planning, he was more used to working with a team. As Mr J expressed it, 'I fell into being an academy head and took over the worst school in the country almost by accident. I knew nothing about academies'.

In a school with a history of truancy and disaffection, he took the bold step to run the Academy with an extended day, from 8.30 to 5 pm, which deliberately included time for doing homework. The day was divided into four two hour lessons with flexible breaks. Minimising lesson changes in the day made it less likely that the students would feel they were on a conveyer belt. 'You want to encourage the teachers to be flexible and creative and make it more interesting because, where you can drill and skill 'em, shut them up, make them do something and kick them out after 45 minutes, you can't do that over two hours with a break in the middle'. This was, as Mr J put it, 'ruthless … and did not give teachers any opt out'.

Certain features of The Marlowe Academy demonstrated the Director's and the business sponsor's commitment to community regeneration. The Innovation Centre, alongside the Academy on the same site, was probably the only one on educational premises outside a university; the library was a community resource and Academy FM, a radio station for Thanet, were both integrated within the Academy building. Both the Innovation Centre and the radio station contributed to the Academy's endeavours; indeed, it was a condition of occupying the Innovation Centre building that time and work experience opportunities would be provided.

THE VALUES OF THE MARLOWE ACADEMY

Mr J expressed these values as:

1. treating people with respect – pupils, parents, teachers
2. supporting each other – to achieve common goals
3. recognising the good in people – bringing that out and creating opportunities for them
4. aiming for ridiculous excellence

In addition, some second order principles implicitly followed including:

5. a curriculum to appeal to students, taught in an interesting way
6. staff and students interacting constantly for social development, community building and surveillance reasons (the last always less explicit but regarded as vital)
7. a flat management structure
8. exploiting the building
9. appropriate staffing mix, staff development and support for staff at all levels
10. designing an education for all, with structural and instructional differentiation
11. engaging the community
12. raising achievement

There was no other school like The Marlowe Academy when it opened. As for the 8.30 to 5.00 school day, it was suggested by a DCSF official that Mr J would close early on the Thursday and the Friday, to which he replied, 'No, that's education by compromise. If we can't teach maths at half past three, four or half past four on a Friday afternoon then we shouldn't be teaching them at all. It should be possible and we should be good enough to do it'. Maybe this was part of the 'ridiculous excellence' referred to.

The rest of this chapter examines how the Academy worked to its stated four values and eight principles in practice, and then reflects on whether this aggregate plan had the potential to succeed with this school in extremely challenging circumstances.

1. Treating people with respect was a central value. Staff should not shout at students (or anyone else) and Mr J modelled this himself with his constant presence around the school. Some of Mr J's non-negotiables were emotional literacy, staff visibility and a non aggressive approach to youngsters; 'As soon as you start shouting at them, the school will begin to fall apart – you absolutely should not model bullying... an abuse of the power and position they [teachers] have. And the kids will do the same'.

The Academy had no bells, whistles or tannoys. The very human, almost family feel about it was evidenced in the availability of staff, most obviously in the open atrium area and at lunch. Getting pupils to move to lessons was accomplished by reminders and mostly friendly chivvying of pupils to where they should be, which, along with assemblies and the two hour lessons, had all been practiced in the old building, making the transfer to the new less disruptive.

The reception of visitors, by whoever, was warm and smiley and parents should not have to wait or make an appointment. The new building attracted other events and these, going on over and above the regular work of the school, were calmly managed. This gave many messages to the young people: this is how we treat strangers; we trust you to be suitably behaved when in public view or otherwise; we are proud of our school.

*2. **Supporting each other*** showed in the spread and shallow hierarchy of the senior management team and in the willingness to pick up quickly on any loudness, running or aggression in the school building. It was everyone's business. It helped that there were three or four staff in middle management at The Ramsgate who were 'good enough to transfer over' to The Marlowe, thereby providing some continuity. It made others who came over from The Ramsgate School feel part of the new school. They could see that people that they had worked with and knew were part of the future. 'You had to be a nutter to work at The Ramsgate School and you had to be committed to work in this community with these children and that is a pretty good starting point for working in the Academy'. As Mr J saw it, 'the rules of the game changed hugely from The Ramsgate to The Marlowe just as it changed hugely from The Ramsgate School before Mr H and Mr C to The Ramsgate School under Mr H and Mr C. What matters is how in tune they are with the core values of the place. The people who came with me from Oxford would have known the values'.

The leadership team was all in place by 1 June, 2005. Four came from Oxford and were known to Mr J as far back as 1990. Mr J saw an understanding of, and signing up to, the vision as more important than simple loyalty. He valued mutual respect and understanding and a solid core of able, senior people within the flat hierarchy.

*3. **Recognising the good in people*** was evident in the very positive approach to pupils, with regular celebration of achievement in the assemblies. Staff were encouraged in their development, from an unemployed mother who was originally a volunteer and was invited to apply for a teaching assistant post and undergo the training that went with it, to a middle manager supported in headship training. More important was the recognition of the children's potential. Growing the sixth form was to help raise aspirations with constant celebration of success.

For decades, the school had had a fearsome reputation. Student teachers would be alarmed when The Ramsgate School was their assigned placement. The behaviour of the pupils was where the problems were seen to lie. That was not the view of those working in The Marlowe. As one senior teacher put it,

> Behaviour is not particularly tough in this school. Literacy is tough. Poor behaviour is a product of weak literacy and poor teaching. You need to be good to teach here. A satisfactory teacher is not good enough here.

Little was made of deprivation and poor levels of education in families, and then not in a judgemental way. The students were the clients, they came from the local area and no attempt was made to bring in a 'better class of pupil' and parent; the job was to teach well those who came to the Academy and adjust organisation and teaching content and style to meet the legitimate care and learning needs of the young people. Respectful behaviour broke out and became rife!

As for the adults, Mr J's outlook was that you have to give people a chance. He had had experience of supporting people 'whose competence is a bit in question' and the initial stance would be:

> There must be something good about this person, so let's see what it is. If you get to the end of the road and it does not work out, then they have to move on. There's any number of people who have left the Academy because they have not fitted in and not been right for this particular context, but have moved on with dignity.

In general, people saw themselves as part of a big team. One teacher said, 'Sometimes I go home thinking I have the best job in the world'.

4. *Aiming for ridiculous excellence*, looking for achievement across a wide front which was beyond the expected, was explicit in this upbeat environment. Mr J was told by the DCSF that the Academy had to reach the national average attainment level of 5A*-Cs in five years. In Chapter 11, the question whether that was a reasonable expectation in a system that included grammar schools is addressed. However, four years on, they were at 64%, just 4% below the 2009 national average. 'People thought we would never do it'. But the government changed the targets: 5 A*-Cs including English and maths became the key indicator in 2009. This was a crude raising of the bar, insensitive to different circumstances.[17] The government had delivered a killer punch! Mr J acknowledged that they had slipped a year behind in pursuit of this goal because they were not ready to start on six hours of maths, six hours of English and two hours a week homework in each of those subjects. From September 2009, 40% of the students' week became English and maths, 16 hours out of 40. 'We could never have done that when we started because the kids would have rebelled, they would have been bored rigid. Now (2010) we are strong enough in our teaching and learning, and the kids and parents have confidence that they can go on to university and get a really good job.'

5. *A curriculum to appeal to students* was part of the initial design where, 'the goal was to make it as interesting and wonderful and as sexy as you can, enriching the curriculum with loads and loads of experiences. The idea was to find things the kids were good at and could progress through'.

The curriculum put in place 'was far more exciting and whizzy and whacky, far more so than it has turned out to be now (2010)'. The curriculum was designed to give youngsters progression routes from 14–19. 'It did work'. Mr J had ruthlessly (the Principal's word) developed the curriculum for the attainment measure at that time. Had the attainment target in 2005 been different, Mr J would have organised the curriculum differently to best meet these requirements. There was an awareness that, in educational leadership, you cannot ignore these imposed benchmarks 'or the young people suffer as do the staff and the school as a whole'. The KS 3 curriculum changed to meet the new requirements. Some of the 'whizziness' had to go. In particular, more time had to be made for mathematics and English. At KS 4, the emphasis on these two subjects increased further.

At the outset in 2005, it was vitally important to get the curriculum right. The Academy did not at that time teach any GCSE courses apart from English, maths and science. The core for KS 4 was four BTEC diploma courses, 12 hours a week: Art and Design, Performing Arts, Travel and Tourism, Business Studies. It worked 'because the students wanted to do it and were given the time to do it really well, and they could achieve four GCSEs and a fifth and sixth if they were clever'.

The extended school day with built in, supervised study periods meant that homework was to be done at these times thus avoiding many of the non-completion of homework problems so common with less academically inclined students when they are expected to do this at home.

6. Staff and students interacting constantly, which was beyond the normal requirements of the job, grew out of the geography of the building and the decisions about how order was to be kept. The open space directly at the entrance was where staff and pupils alike could get snacks, eat and chat together, including with people from the Innovation Centre. From there, students were ushered to lessons and were met at the classroom door in a culture of respect and cooperation. The modelling of behaviour from all adults was clear.

7. The flatly distributed management structure remained, though roles changed over six years. The leadership team consisted of 13 staff, including the Principal. The Principal noted that, as the school got larger, so involvement on his part with individuals reduced. Originally he had interviewed all the staff for The Marlowe. He had talked to them all individually about where they saw themselves going and what The Marlowe might offer them. In the first two or three years, he continued to have regular, close personal involvement with all the staff, even with individual learning mentors and teaching assistants. He was still doing this in 2011, but it made things like assemblies, staff briefings and wandering round the school more difficult. As a result, team leaders became more important to him.

Members of the senior leadership team had great autonomy: there was no assistant head or deputy looking over their shoulders. All had a part to play in supporting the overall development of the Academy, explicitly stated in their JD. 'It is the whole team who would feel gutted if the English results were not up to scratch.' The leadership team members were 'bubbles around the centre rather than a pyramid', each with a further circle of bubbles around them – fanciful as this may seem. What was evident was the commitment of a leadership team of 13 to the model established by Mr J. It was larger than the core team under Mr H, but had as much solidarity, acted in unity and spoke with one voice in the same way.

8. *Exploiting the building* influenced the way the Academy was organised. Showing local head teachers around, Mr J heard these colleagues say they would never choose to run a school with the high walkways – a health and safety disaster area as they saw it. For Mr J it was another opportunity to force staff into close proximity to students, to be available and visible, and to interact. While this was ostensibly for safety purposes, it coincided with Mr J's wish to break down the barriers between adults and students. He was always around and senior staff were out on the balconies at break-time. Teachers were encouraged to stand at the classroom door and greet children as they arrived for a class.

The Principal occupied an open plan space on the first floor, much like the upper deck of a ship, jutting out into the open space. Students dropped in all the time. It was more than an open door policy: there was no door. As Mr J said, 'The Marlowe could not run if staff were not taking responsibility all day'. The open area was one ingredient for breaking down barriers. At the outset, in the old building, they had created a central space in which to operate the same way for safety, surveillance and community building. Surveillance was happening without people knowing it. In the new building, there were few corners where students could hide away and misbehave. The back stairs was one and locks were put on these which could be sprung open from a central switch in an emergency.

More positively, the building was the most powerful statement. It stood out, made the point that the local population was valued and that it was for them. People from the Newington estate mattered and a huge investment was being made in the education of their young people. It was a flagship, beacon, award-winning building, looked after meticulously with repainting every half term, costed into the original budget, and carpets replaced regularly.

In the old building, where the Academy had spent its first year, every wall was painted white and chairs were sorted and moved so that every classroom had chairs of the same colour rather than a random mix. It seemed overly fussy but it gave the right message about order, and caring for the pupils' surroundings. Overall, with the extended school day going on until 5pm, even in the old building, it was a huge change in the social environment.

9. *Appropriate staffing mix, staff development and support for staff at all levels* were key parts of The Marlowe's operation. In September 2009, the staffing for this school of 823 students totalled 245 people. This included 87 teachers and two graduate trainees, 85 teaching assistants, 40 administrative and clerical staff and 31 maintenance workers. This differed hugely in scale and variety of roles compared with the staffing figures for 1986. Recruitment was not easy, particularly for English, maths and science. It was difficult to get quality people in these areas and maths and science had always been shortage subjects anyway. Every Tuesday 8–10 am was set aside for staff development. The Principal recognised that, 'It is more difficult to teach well here than it is in other schools – the levels of need, the range of ability. You have to be very, very good to get the levels of learning that these students require.'

The staff development included, for some, training in classroom observation and assessment, Ofsted style, and their assessments were validated by practising Ofsted inspectors so they would know where they stood in terms of Ofsted grading. Staff were observed formally up to six times in a year. It was all tabulated and reviewed. They had coaching, training, curriculum reviews and teachers had their excellence portfolios: 'You name it, we are on to it.'

10. Designing an education for all with structural and instructional differentiation was led by Mrs F. Her title was Student Support and Guidance, with responsibility for Special Educational Needs, EAL, Careers Advice, liaising with outside agencies, child protection and looked after children (children in the care of the local authority). Dealing with students' learning difficulties and their social and health needs was an essential and labour-intensive part of the work of the Academy. It could not be dealt with in the traditional way with a SENCO, small scale interventions and a little one to one support. The numbers were just too great, always more than 40% of the school population and in 2011 over 50% (see Table 7.1). The complex SEN set up, which is described in more detail in the next chapter, became more sophisticated as needs emerged. Mrs F's approach had always been to identify what could be the blocks to student learning, whether it was a social communication issue, mental health, welfare or a combination of difficulties. Often the blocks were not identified until secondary education by which time children have been traumatised by their struggles – 'just treated as naughty children'.

The school population had grown and with it the numbers with these sorts of difficulty. So, in 2010, the MAAC (Marlowe Assessment and Achievement Centre) replaced a very short term holding area for difficult incidents and outreach, in-class support to a separate centre, longer stays and an alternative to fixed period exclusions. This was almost certainly a response to the greater pressures to raise standards, both for teachers and students. There was less scope for being relaxed about work being done, or isolated behaviour flare-ups being dealt with calmly, with the objective of maintaining the student in the class.

The Marlowe was supported hugely by the other services in the area, educational and others: social services around child protection issues; extra Connexions time because raising aspirations was vital; speech and language therapy; fostering agencies; sports clubs, Breakthrough CAMHS, other health agencies. and voluntary organisations. There were also places commissioned at the FE college, for KS 4 students who were 'past the point where they could work sensibly here';

The inclusion effort was part of raising standards for all. For four years, the Academy was doing well in terms of attainment and maybe there should have been a greater and earlier focus on literacy, more even than the accelerated reading scheme provided. However, Mrs F found it rewarding working at The Marlowe, in partnership with the Principal who had all the qualities she would want to see in a leader. She knew she could do the job she wanted to do. She described her team as, 'outstanding, professional and committed people and there is always someone for a frazzled team member to turn to'.

11. Engaging the community was vital from the outset, part even of the thinking of the Director who felt that, without community regeneration, standards would not rise. Quite what the school's role in community regeneration would look like when fully implemented was not clear. There were plans for a 'One Stop Shop', which did not happen. Although not in the education budget, the community library was established in the school. At this time the County was developing a community school strategy for which The Marlowe Academy could have been a model, if fully – and expensively – funded.

Mr J was always available to visitors and parents and the latter were all given his mobile number. 'There are one or two families that are struggling with us, but the vast majority appreciate what we are doing and appreciate the change. If someone phones up with a complaint, you go out and sort it.' He only received about one call a week on the mobile. If they drop in, it was Mr S's role (Academy manager) to meet and greet. They are not sent away with the reason that, sorry we have not got time to deal with this today.

The assemblies were obviously celebratory events for the internal community and annual events like Marlowe Academy World Awareness Day (MAWAD) did much to generate acceptance of 'difference'. Staff from different countries had prepared food and Afghani boys were dancing. Racial incidents that did occur were dealt with very sternly; one nasty incident between Afghani boys and 'white kids reacting badly' resulted in five permanent exclusions.

The Innovation Centre, the community library on site, Academy FM radio and use of the school building for community events were further developments. Links with local primary schools were strong, partly of course for the recruitment motive. Conferences from time to time took place in the school during term time with no nervousness on the part of school staff and participants joined students in the dining area for lunch. Arguably, more could have been done to reach out to families and promote activities for local people. Without strenuous outreach efforts, real involvement of parents is not generated.

12. Raising achievement was a vital goal, which could never be compensated for by a warm community feel and great social care. A secondary school is expected to make three levels of progress from KS 2 to 4. Fisher Family Trust calculations, based on intake characteristics and prior attainment, predicted for 2011 that 22% of Year 11s would gain 5A*-C grades that included maths and English. This would put the Academy in the top 25% performing schools. Student numbers grew over the six years, great effort to raise attendance worked and attainment levels increased over that period.

The Principal made it plain that you could not blame the quality of the students and there was a heartening reticence to bring this up as an excuse, partly because the Academy was to stand as a service to the neighbourhood, accept its clientele and its job to provide the appropriate teaching and support for young people to learn and, moreover, to catch up. Its value-added was good year on year for attainment between KS 2 and KS 4 as shown in table 7.1.

Table 7.1. Marlowe Academy Contextual Value Added (CVA)

Year	All subjects	English	Maths
2006	990.1	998.6	1002.3
2007	1013.5	999.4	999.3
2008	1035.3	1002.1	1004.0
2009	1006.6	998.2	1001.2
2010	1005.1	997.2	1001.0
2011	958.7	994.2	999.2

CVA has as its mean 1,000. Anything above this is performing beyond the mean, but the error margins can be fairly large.

THE NEWINGTON PHEONIX

The design for the Academy, approved by the trustees, was determinedly and self-confidently set out by Mr J. It resulted in huge differences in the relationships and management compared with the previous regimes. All agreed there was a transformation; it was a different kind of place, even in the first year in the old building. The phoenix, rising out of past difficulties, was developing and producing results on very many levels. It was a negotiated, planned, gradualist model which took account of student characteristics and staffing capabilities and was on an upward trajectory continuing into 2011. All this was put in jeopardy by the Ofsted 'notice to Improve' delivered in October 2010.

The principles driving the Academy and the structures put in place were designed to produce some improvements and successfully did this. The positive atmosphere and good relationships made more pupils want to attend and managing behaviour kept exclusions down compared with the Academy's predecessor schools. The whizziness of the curriculum and the supportive style, for staff and students, may not have fitted the increasing centrist demands of the English education system. Literacy levels were a particular problem and reports suggested the gap between reading age and chronological age actually increased as students moved from KS 3 to KS 4. The values-based leadership was not consonant with a results-focussed drive to raise levels. The compromises which Mr J made may not have been enough to satisfy inspectors, the DfE or trustees. This is taken up further in Chapter 9.

THE MARLOWE ACADEMY – ACTION, REACTION AND IMPACT

A NEW CULTURE AND ANOTHER NEW BEGINNING

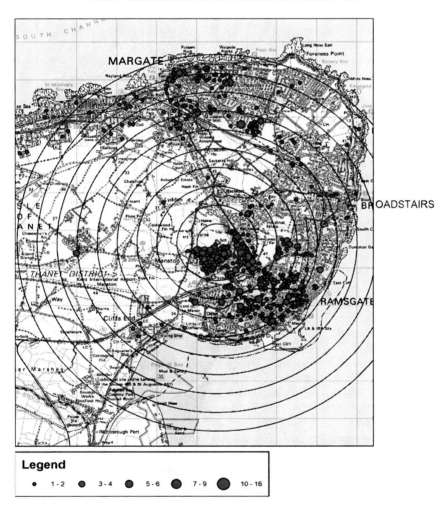

Figure 8.1. Distribution of students attending The Marlowe Academy 2009.

The Academy is located at the centre of the concentric circles in Figure 8.1. The close clustering of the home locations of students is evident with some coming also from the more difficult areas of Margate to the north. Thanet as a whole is the parson's nose out on a limb with sea on three sides with accessibility problems that contributed to unemployment and made teacher recruitment difficult, the more so in challenging schools.

The sections of this chapter describe, firstly, the initial year in the old building, followed by coverage of the whole period in terms of: atmosphere and relationships; the assemblies as a means of developing cohesion; staff and staffing; lessons and learning; special needs; and results. The last section reflects on six years of The Marlowe Academy in action, how it was judged against national government standards applied, through Ofsted and HM Inspectorate.

THE FIRST YEAR

The Academy's first year of operation in The Ramsgate school building was described as exciting and challenging. There was a feeling in the local community that things were changing with a new building going up, and there was, reportedly, nervousness from the other local head teachers about the disturbance to the educational landscape in which they had previously functioned comfortably.

One observer reported that the 'feel' was immediately different, that there was a lot more pride and that there was a sense that they were educating the whole person, building confidence and a love of learning, raising aspirations, 'a hub of learning for the community'. And that was in the old building! There had been a recruitment drive when the Academy was due to open: new beginning, new building and new style were quite a draw. 'We got some incredibly good staff. They were in the classrooms delivering high quality teaching'. The first year was a very hopeful, happy time with lots of the innovation and fine-tuning.

There were lots of hearts and minds to win in that first year, with staff doing things like no other school in the country, 'and you would not bet on the students wanting to be there 'til 5 o'clock, really'. It was a huge change and a tough first year. Mr J recalls having parents coming to shout at him, 'because that was what they were used to'. Changing the culture and ethos inside the school and in relationships with the community was as hard as expected. They had had a year practicing the new regime, new relationships, new timetables, new curricula and whole school assemblies; the new building was made for whole school assemblies with its huge atrium area. In assemblies, Mr J acknowledged a necessary sequence: first, entertain to gain attention, then educate.

The Academy was to become the sort of place where you did not just turn up to be lectured and droned at; there was a bit of humour, contributions from a range of different people and a myriad of activities and opportunities. The community spirit became cemented during this first year in the old building. They even watched the world cup matches on the big screen in the old school. It was not about being repressed or compressed together and staff and students could laugh together at the same things.

In the new building, 'it was never going to be about bullying and repressing them'. It was to be about encouragement, motivation and getting success. The view was that you were never going to get the students to value the new building, respect it and respect each other if you did not do that yourself. The no-shouting, calm approach to discipline, and expectations that all staff would be available for as much of the day as possible was unwritten yet palpably present in the new Academy.

THE ATMOSPHERE AND RELATIONSHIPS

The atmosphere at The Marlowe was sustained by senior staff and carried over to the new building, with the curriculum and routines which had been established in the 1960s structure, which was demolished in months. The Principal's day was regularly 12 or 13 hours. He was around the school constantly. Paperwork and other administrative necessities would be done before the start of the school day. If he had no meetings, he would be out and about monitoring and supporting – or just wandering around, checking, having conversations, seeing how the building work was going. He had a list of incidental things he wanted to achieve during the day, often a chat to a series of people about specific things. There was a lot of looking for good things to praise and reinforce, not looking for problems and chasing solutions. There was a view that emphasising the good things could avoid problems, or some of them, and the subsequent damage repair work that would then be required. Mr J acknowledged that one did point out the bad things, 'as many as a person can bear to hear', but the emphasis had to be, in terms of his style, personality and beliefs, on 'what is fab'.

What one might see at the start of the day, as students arrived, were easy-going exchanges between staff and students. Around one table would be the ASD base group seemingly getting comfortable with each other, the ASD staff and whatever the day had to offer. It was like a big family of 12 around a breakfast table, a long way from an institutional feel. Yet institution it was, housing nearly 900 pupils and over 200 staff with assorted tasks and objectives.

With the student body of the Marlowe, there needed to be a new approach involving calm, respectful relations, and a vast amount of informal support and guidance work that had to be undertaken to support the teaching of the formal curriculum. Examples are given below, some of which would be a rare sight in secondary schools

At the mid morning break, a girl, aged about 13, came to stand by one table where teachers were seated talking and, as invariably happened when a pupil approached, the teacher she wanted to speak to turned away from colleagues and gave her full attention to the girl. The girl quite unselfconsciously stroked teacher's ringlets with several slow sweeps of her hand while talking softly. The teacher responded to her socially and reassuringly with no reaction to the hair-stroking. The girl, while not smiling, was relaxed and it was unusual to see this physical touching and the acceptance, indeed, seeming unawareness of it so natural was it. Miss P explained later that the girl was in her tutor group and until recently had not engaged at all, no eye contact, no conversation. There came a point where Miss P judged she could push through and engage insistently with the girl; she took the risk and the girl had responded positively.

Other pleasant social interactions, not possible without this communal concourse, included a girl coming past Mr L, and as she passed, she put up her hand and they did the hand slap, touching fingers and pressing knuckles routine. A boy came up to one of the senior team members explaining that he had altered the powerpoint presentation for assembly in two days time. 'I was up all night miss. My computer was red hot.' They high-fived and she promised to look at the powerpoint in the afternoon and get back to him the next morning.

There was a lot of movement during the morning mid-lesson break. Mr S was active making sure that movement on the raised area, where there were 40+ children, did not get too boisterous. In the space below there were the tables, many with children and adults sitting together. S, the PCSO, seemed on this particular morning to spend a lot of time at the front door, the single point of exit. She explained that, 'It annoys me that kids keep getting out'. She would then get calls to say kids were throwing stones or there was damage or shoplifting so this was about preventing offences – and forcing them to stay in and continue learning.

During this break period also, Mr T. and three other adults were at a table with a girl seemingly in a sulk. They were giving her much encouragement. After some while, the mother left and hugged the girl who went with Mr T to sell cakes and sweets at a makeshift stall set up there as part of a charitable fund-raising event.

Sitting in the open area, S (PCSO) was having 'a bit of a go' at one Year 8 boy, telling him that one of the teachers should not have to put up with his bad behaviour. Another is also contributing calling him 'love', 'darlin' whilst telling him off.

Mr T was a counsellor trained in dynamic therapy and did work on emotional intelligence. One of his 'lads' from the Brothers group of at risk boys came by looking for M, the youth worker. When he eventually arrived they had an enthusiastic conversation about a camping trip, apparently suggested by the Brothers. The Brothers group and the separate Sisters group catered for groups who might be excluded. The groups worked at self esteem and anger management.

Still in the mid morning break, there was a disciplinary incident: a student was sent out from a session. He was shocked. 'I am being sent home already'. He had been talking to a friend, and been told to leave the classroom because it was not his teaching group. His response was to swear, as he described it, 'I swore around her (the teacher) not at her'. The youth worker talked to him. Two teachers joined the group to ask the student the details. The youth worker eventually helped him give an account of the incident, actually writing it for him.

M, the youth worker and S, the PCSO, had taken about a dozen pupils camping – volunteer children and those who had been targeted. S dealt with child protection and domestic violence and was the liaison with whatever appropriate sections needed to be contacted at the police station. It was the school's decision to employ her and she was 50% funded by the school and 50% by the police service. She saw it very much as prevention but acknowledged that she could also, when required, play the enforcer role. She worked with 13–16 year old girls in the Sisters group, whom she referred to as 'young ladies' The group had their own budget and arranged activities. She could see lots of improvement, especially in self esteem, to which they devoted a lot of effort. Asked if she 'just did X or Y…', she replied forcefully, 'I don't *just* do anything – I will do anything I have to do, all sorts of things to support the youngsters, talking to them, helping them to do make-up, CV's, getting a pregnancy test ….'.

In the open area, as children were leaving, a boy was with a teacher who was looking quite severe. The boy had not done his work. He began by looking slightly truculent, a bit of a smile. He was asked where his English work was. At home. He was asked to show his timetable. Asked why other homework had not been done, he said he was not given any. Apparently it was given and was on a piece of paper but he had not been attentive enough. He was to bring the work to Mr J on Monday morning. If he had a problem and could not do it then he must go to see Mr J earlier. Mr J concluded with: 'Mrs W thinks I am being soft. If this does not work it's going to be parents in and a big discussion. You and I are going to fall out and it will take a long time to overcome that.' The boy by this time had lost the smile and looked serious, even worried.

The Academy FM studio is alongside the open area with a window looking onto the internal space. The manager said, 'I love being in the school. Mr J is an absolute star. His vision for education is incredible. He inspires me. If we can find another way to help kids get through then that is good. It is part of why we are here'.

He told the story of Will, brought in by his year head as a student who was not engaging in any way. He simply seemed to be shut! The boy would turn up to the studio every Tuesday morning but sit without engaging, however jolly people were about him. The studio manager decided to take him into the studio and asked Will to read out a piece he had prepared. He did it very quietly. At the end, Will said, 'I liked that'. The manager raised the pressure, asking him what was wrong and gradually broke through to find he was bullied because of his ethnicity and looks. He reported to Mr J who reported onto the year head and within minutes there was incredible support put around the young person. This was SO impressive, as the studio manager saw it. 'Will's story went through me like a hot knife through butter. It was so rewarding what I achieved with Will'. He then asked Will to write something about the experience of being bullied because there are probably several students at other schools who feel the same.

Surveillance in the Academy building was also important and could not always be light-hearted and friendly. Mr R was in the computer area catching up on work on the computer. Mr S came by and said that 6th formers without kit were mucking around and he wanted them outside in the cold. They should have come with their kit. They should be doing games and, if they were not, he wanted them to feel the alternative was not a better option.

At the end of day, Mr J was at the gate with two members of staff and said they had a very jokey relationship which was good for the students to see. They did not stand there simply to police the exit. In fact, when it was suggested that they were 'on patrol' the response was, 'No, just winding down after a busy day'. As one teacher said, everyone assumed that The Marlowe was a war zone, but that insiders knew it was not. Another reported his resentment at outsiders saying to him, 'So, are you wearing your flak jacket today?'

Asked about the existence of an Inclusion Unit or 'punishment block', the Principal said, 'There is no punishment facility here; it would go against our philosophy'. Most staff accepted this and that if an 'inclusion unit' (really an *ex*clusion room) were opened, it would be filled and give permission to label some children as punishable or deserving punishment. One member of the support team was positively disposed towards the need for such a unit at the end of a particularly trying, being-shouted-at day but it *seemed* a minority view.

ASSEMBLIES, COHESION AND LEARNING

Mr J said, 'I thought hard about whole school assemblies. Twice a week from the beginning. Yes, I had to look them in the eye and insist'. He had carefully prepared inputs and had talked to the staff and made it clear he could not do this by himself. They were to sit with their students. He talked to the students and did not shout at them and berate them. Ultimately, it was about facing down a small number of students and making them understand that this was an important time and that he had put time into preparing this for them.

Prior to one assembly, few staff were in evidence; most were probably at the staff briefing. Mr R and Mr S were patrolling but it was all very gentle. Staff appeared, many doing the registers which they carried around looking to see who was there and ticking them off. Children settled a bit. Mr S, wired for sound, called for quiet, several times, in a relatively quiet, certainly non-shouting way and staff moved amongst the children; there was a hush and Mr J took over.

He talked about literacy, a Year 7 debate about the X factor and, 'Do footballers get paid too much?' He said that literacy was about all sorts of understanding and he was going to talk about current affairs regularly. Today he was going to tell them things that were in the Sunday newspapers, well, one Sunday newspaper, *The Observer*.

A colleague projected the stories on the screen as he referred to them. He went through: global warming, hospitals with significantly high death rates, difficulties young people will have in getting mortgages, Mr Gove, Secretary of State for Education, and his plans for schools, the FIFA scandal of the voting on the 2018 world cup football location and the Panorama programme that would report on it. He emphasised how much of this was relevant to them, either immediately or in the near future. He reflected on his uncertainty about how many of them read newspapers at any point in the week but encouraged them to see the relevance to them. One could ask about how much of the material was going in but it was an exposure that an educator felt to be important.

Mr J recalled an assembly in the first year which was significant. It was on the Armenian earthquake. He played music – *Remember Me*, Alyson Moyet – and every time she sang that line a new image came up. There was a stunned silence at the end of that assembly. The suggestion that they raise money for this disaster resulted in £300 or £400.

A turning point in Mr J's mind, had been when a rumour went around that a nearby school was going to raid The Marlowe. The students were unsettled, milling around at afternoon break and it was difficult to get on with the work of education until 5pm. The Principal had the challenge the next day of deciding what to say. He could have given them all a good telling off, but the way he approached it was to say,

'I'm really disappointed at the way you behaved yesterday afternoon. There was so little learning going on. What really gutted me about yesterday was that you were not using your brains'. They all looked at him and he continued, 'Do you really think X school have got the bottle to come up here and take us on?'

A risky strategy to be sure. There was a three second pause and then everybody, staff and students, burst out laughing. It was a recurring joke in that first year and part of establishing the sense of a new identity.

In 2010, Mr J's assembly on Turkey included his holiday snaps, information about Turkey's failed attempts to join the EU and religion. Graphs were projected to make the points about differences in temperature between Thanet and Anatolia and a photograph of an ancient inscription was shown that looked like the Marlowe Academy logo!

Mr J's assemblies became legends, taking two or three hours to produce. Whole school assemblies were fundamental to the Academy, entertaining but also a time when they all came together, praised people and showed what was good. They were a contribution to and demonstration of the school community's cohesion, and an opportunity to teach, to introduce the whole school to material and ideas they might not otherwise encounter. At the same time, there were messages about appropriate and inappropriate behaviour, things to celebrate and inspire – and some humour.

STAFF AND STAFFING

The staff body worked very hard. Lots of them saw themselves as part of the solution, coaching and supporting colleagues. Where people struggled, there was lots of support. 'The best teacher in the world who felt unsupported would struggle'. Where individuals were not up to it, they were eased out in a fair way, with dignity. As the Principal said, some fall by the wayside and ten teachers left in the 2010/11 academic year. There was a hard edge to staff planning and the decisions had to be made early enough in the school year, by January, if the best NQTs were to be recruited. The Academy was successful in the spring of 2011 in its recruitment and was fully staffed for September 2011.

The other side of this staff management responsibility, as described by Mr J, was that in this climate and with these challenges it would be possible to get things wrong and push staff too far to the extent that morale dips. A sophistication of leadership was needed in this challenging situation.

Mr P saw the orderliness of students in the Academy as the result of lots of hard work and gentle cajoling. His Year 10 and 11s, he said, were horrible at the start of the year, but he had 'only to look at them now'. He dropped in on The Marlowe where they needed a long term supply teacher. He was on his way to another school but thought as he walked up to the new building, 'What am I doing? This is the Ramsgate School', but he never left. He fell in love with the place, he said.

Another, who arrived after three years' experience elsewhere, reported that this was his home area and he wanted to come back to teach in this school in this kind of community but only after he had got some experience under his belt. He said,

> The first four months were the hardest experience in all my career. I felt isolated and powerless in the classroom. The flexible breaks in the long lessons made it harder. There were no sanctions really and my previous school had been quite macho, but in this one shouting was no good because they could shout louder. You had to build up relationships and that meant meeting the students in different places and working in more subtle ways outside classroom, talking to students socially. You have to want to be here.

However, despite these positive comments, it became gradually more difficult to recruit, much more so after the negative inspection of autumn of 2010. Then the Academy struggled to keep teachers who did come. The gleam of newness had gone, and meeting the requirement that 35% of the students should reach national standards meant that innovation and whizziness had declined. As one teacher said, 'In the beginning lots of things were different about the Academy, but, over time, we have become more like other schools except that there are no bells and we stay until five o'clock.' Some faculties had to work with teachers not trained in the relevant subject or whose teaching qualification was for a different level.

Mr J said, 'My best teachers don't have behaviour problems. It is because the kids are interested, they are engaged, they are active, they are participating, they want to get up to the next level, they feel valued. And a good teacher will engender good behaviour. It is not "behaviour"; it is learning behaviour'. Nonetheless, after five years and little public recognition of how far they had come, some staff were asking how long they could continue in such a demanding environment, even though they were committed and had faith in the students' ability to achieve.

LESSONS AND LEARNING

When the new routines had become established, Mr J was able to recall, 'Then I was not fire-fighting all the time. I was still fire-fighting, but not all the time. I was around and about all day, every day because I would be modelling for everyone what I felt was the right approach. And if they did not see me doing it they would never know what the expectations were'.

One Friday afternoon, in this early period, a teacher came to him in tears saying it was not working and that the school was falling apart. He suggested they go round, 3–5 pm on that Friday afternoon, with a clipboard and go into every lesson and she was to give a tick or a cross as to whether things were working; it was all ticks except for one. The conclusion was that, even late on a Friday, it was working. That was quite important and that would help to spread the message. With flexible breaks and students around all the time, it was not easy but the lessons were going reasonably well, the students were on board and it was coming together.

For two days I tracked first a Year 10 and then a Year 11 class. My main focus was on the extent of engagement of the pupils and the smooth running of lessons and change-overs. I was looked after by Charlotte, a student, when following the Year 10s.

In a maths lesson with 24 students. Charlotte said apologetically to me, 'Excuse the noise, but this is not our usual teacher' – and it seemed their books were locked in a cupboard. The lead maths subject mentor came in to brief the class. They were to do their work in their study books. The register was taken and there was soon quiet working. There was a list of six students on the board who had had to borrow pens. The maths subject mentor was later managing the lunch queue, squirting the antiseptic liquid on the hands of all those passing. 'I love my job!' she said as I got my squirt – she was referring to her subject and pastoral roles.

Humanities with 26 students was led by a student teacher but in effect team taught. She had on the board 'media and prejudice' and the learning objective was 'to understand the role the media plays in portraying youth'. The student teacher spent a fair bit of time demanding silence – which did not last. When the teacher took over and talked about emotive writing giving examples the students were attentive. 'People have talked about The Marlowe and Newington in negative ways. You are pre-judged'. He asked what they could do to change opinions, remarking that they were now orderly and thanking them. One student offered the view that The Marlowe was judged by how the old Ramsgate school was. 'Has it got better?' 'Yes', But another pupil said that it was the same school in the same place.

An ICT class was outside doing time-lapse photography. Most of the class were in groups enjoying the changing positions as the camera person (teacher to begin with and then 6th formers) counted down to the next shot. The session finished with the young people sitting in a snake formation and after each shot the back one moved to the front to give the impression of a snake slithering forward.

In a mixed **Year 10 maths** class, fairly large at 24 students, Mrs S maintained a fast pace. She did several examples and the students were visibly keen to both get it right and understand it. Some of the students were impressively quick. Mrs S said later that in a previous lesson one lad had asked a question which surprised her; she could not believe he had not 'got it'. The student thought she was putting him down, packed his bag and walked out saying, 'jog on'. It showed how sensitive they could be and she did not treat it as a disciplinary matter but a pastoral concern.

In this **mixed history class**, Mr L spoke very loudly, jokily and colloquially with the students. The topic was 'sustainable cities' and a later stimulus input was on surveillance in cities illustrated with a UTube film. There was lots of seemingly incidental chat, but students kept working in between contributing to the conversation eg about *Facebook*. The atmosphere was very amiable, with the discussion closely or more distantly related to the topic.

A Year 10 top set English class of 17 girls was managed by a young female teacher supported by a teaching assistant. The focus was on oracy and the task was to develop an argument related to Katie Price, aka Jordan. The students were to work out a position on whether Jordan should have joined the reality TV programme *I'm a celebrity get me out of here* while her small son was in hospital. The resource was a graphic and stimulating video of an interview with Jordan and various shots of her taking part in reality TV programmes. After a little explanation by the teacher, two girls immediately got into an argument about Jordan and her reputation. The argument got louder and more energetic, one saying Jordan was great and no one should criticize her while the other was saying she was a slag and should be at home looking after her sick son. The young teacher could not quell this energy and a teacher from next door came in. He tried quietly to settle them. The head of English came in and tried similarly. Finally Mister S, the Academy Manager, arrived as the ultimate disciplinary force. He simply said, 'Come with me, please', beckoned the main protagonist with his hand and repeated his request several times. It was met by, 'Why me? It was them as well. It's always me'. The girl left the room with Mister S. What should not be overlooked is that 13 girls sat waiting patiently, presumably understanding that, no matter what their feelings about Jordan, the task was about developing and presenting an argument. Mister S said later the girl had been sent home, 'not something I like to do'. The teacher was able to joke at the end about how they would have reacted had they been debating something more serious, like the Arab-Israeli conflict.

In the lessons I saw, there was variability in the responsiveness of the pupils to their teachers. Sometimes this related to the time of day. About half were *sustained workers*. Other groups could be designated *dedicated talkers*, the *intermittent unstretched* and the odd *compulsive walker*. It required good teachers to hold pupils' attention, demonstrate the right amounts of flexibility and responsiveness and maintain relationships. Those students who did not fall into the crudely labelled *sustained workers* category were essentially playing, as young people will. To turn them into workers, even for short bursts, could be challenging. Most of all, it was clear that relationships and authority were not built up quickly but grew and were earned as teachers prepared, taught and fed back to students. The challenge to entertain *and* educate was demanding at The Marlowe. Recognising the energy and fun in young people, one would not want it crushed.

SPECIAL EDUCATIONAL NEEDS

Special educational needs provision, defined broadly, was an essential part of The Marlowe where, as shown in Table 8.1, 50% of the pupils were registered as having some level of special need. Provision for six years was as integrated as it could be and was adjusted to meet the social *as well as* the educational needs of children in a high poverty area. It is a matter of judgement and ideology as to whether the balance was right. Ms F, the senior leadership team member for Support and Guidance, recognised that the staff had been through hard times and were not initially expecting the 'new lot' to last beyond half term.

Taking students *off* the special needs register was one criterion for judging a school, but in the case of The Marlowe there were some children who had enduring, severe and complex needs. There was the growing expectation generally in education that identifying a student with SEN would result in a period of focussed input after which the difficulty would be overcome and they could be taken off the register.[18] Marlowe looked and felt like a successful school but it did not fit the normal profile with its results continuing to be so low. Yet it succeeded at so many levels. Mrs F said with a passion, 'It is the most successful school I have been in, the most successful in raising their ambitions and helping them develop from where they are.' That this was not reflected in sufficiently improved literacy levels was not necessarily a damning judgement.

The student welfare office was next to *family liaison*. Together they had a staff of six, a number of whom had worked in the Academy and predecessor schools for 15 years, committed local people, dedicated to that community. 'It is obvious that what we have here is special', with children first and systems described as 'elastic'. They worked with a number of external agencies concerned with parents, child protection, disabled, medical or distressed and internally liaise well with the support and guidance team. The Marlowe, it was felt, could manage in-house many of the problems which other schools may have referred elsewhere. They had two social work assistants whose roles were preventative and involved going out to families to help them set up strategies for dealing with youngsters who were beginning to be problematic. Around 20 families in a year benefited from this service. They conducted six to eight week long courses for 20 or 30 parents at a time. A group of regular parent volunteers also contributed.

The family liaison officer engaged in a friendly way with parents, seeing that as more likely to gain support for education from them. There were also examples of good-natured confrontation. She recounted how one parent had said that education had never been of much use to him and its lack had never done him any harm. She retorted that he hadn't got a job, that he had admitted to not being able to read a newspaper and that he had told how he had been fiddled out of money because his maths wasn't very good. And did he want that for his own child? She admitted 'sailing close to the wind' on some occasions, but parents and carers knew she wanted the best for them and their children.

The ASD (Autistic Spectrum Disorder) base, with its seven staff and over 60 students, aimed to get them into mainstream classrooms with support packages. She said they had to know the children well, what their needs were and what would set them off. If a lesson caused anxiety, they might accompany the child or the child brought work back to the base. The aim was to gradually increase students' time in the classroom, 'get them educated and to be happy'.

Cliffsend, the EBD unit, was run by Mr D, who saw its role as supporting students in class wherever possible, keeping them in mainstream, ensuring they were in school as much as possible and that they were learning. For 2011/12, the MAAC (Marlowe Assessment and Achievement Centre) was planned for up to 20 youngsters who were having series of fixed term exclusions and others for whom they had no other strategy except to reduce their timetable.

Three staff, line managed by Mr D, were out and about monitoring and recording. They had parental contact, used CAMHS (Child and Adolescent Mental Health Service) and the youth intervention scheme. Exam success was something they sought but it was not the prime goal. One of the team expressed a strongly held view that these students had done better at the Marlowe than if they had not been in this school. 'The vast majority would not survive in mainstream beyond Year 7.' It was estimated that three quarters of the students from the unit were in mainstream classes for 50% of the time. Some had poor attendance and it was very challenging to actually get the most disaffected into school.

The Academy was responsive and designed provision to meet need; some students had caring responsibilities for younger siblings, so the Academy set up an after school club for the younger siblings to come to at the end of their day in neighbouring primary schools. This enabled the Marlowe students to finish their school day without worry.

Maintaining the point of balance between pressuring students to achieve and keeping the Academy a pleasant, inclusive environment that students wanted to attend was a deliberate, principle-driven decision. However, the push for excellence in the provision of guidance and support was not accompanied by excellence in other areas. Assessment of student progress was considered by one set of external reviewers, commissioned by the trustees in 2011, to be less systematic than it might be. Support staff were judged to be poorly focussed on the individual learning requirements of special needs students, and variable standards of planning and marking were also criticised. These factors were all thought to be associated with a lower than hoped for average rate of progress in learning – and the consequent shortfall compared with national floor targets. Specifically on literacy interventions, monitoring was judged inadequate and the lack of progress in pupils' literacy between the ages of 11 and 16 was registered as a cause for concern.

RESULTS

The Marlowe Academy achieved continuous improvement in its results at 16. It cannot be stated too strongly that the children attending were recognisably the same as those 10 years before, with the same tendency to lose concentration, the same potential for conflict, the same levels of deprivation as indicated by free school meals entitlement rates and the same 50% proportion identified as having special educational needs. Free school meal rates were approaching twice the national average and SEN rates two and a half times the national average with statemented children at a similar highly disproportionate level.

Table 8.1. GCSE attainment, numbers on role, SEN and FSM 2006–2011*

	The Marlowe Academy					Nationally			
Year	*No. on Roll*	*% 5A*-C GCSEs*	*% 5A*-C GCSEs inc M & Eng*	*% SEN*	*% Free School Meals*	*% 5A*-C GCSEs*	*% 5A*-C GCSEs inc M & Eng*	*% SEN*	*% Free School Meals***
2006	559	28	5	54.4 (2.9)	34.9	*59*	*44*	*17.6*	*13.1*
2007	677	39	7	51.4 (2.8)	31.5	*60*	*46*	*18.5*	*14.4*
2008	738	52	13	43.9 (3.1)	29.4	*64*	*48*	*19.9*	*14.2*
2009	777	64	12	45.2 (3.9)	33.8	*68*	*50*	*21.1*	*14.5*
2010	823	68	14	46.5 (4.9)	33.7	*75*	*54*	*21.7*	*15.4*
2011	872	63	20	51.1 (5.1)	34.7	*79*	*57*	*20.6*	*15.9*

*Most of the data taken from the Academy's RAISEonline files **State funded secondary schools

Numbers on roll increased each year. What was also evident was the slight increase of students coming from the local area as shown in Figure 8.2. It showed that, going up through the compulsory school years from NC years 7 to 11, the more recent entrants came from closer to the school. Over 60% of Years 7 and 8, ie those entering the school in 2008 and 2009, came from within 2km of the Academy compared with 50% in Year 11. The Marlowe Academy had not pursued the fairly common academy strategy of looking for a new and more affluent intake to boost its results. It had focussed its recruitment on the local Newington, Whitehall and Highfields estates.

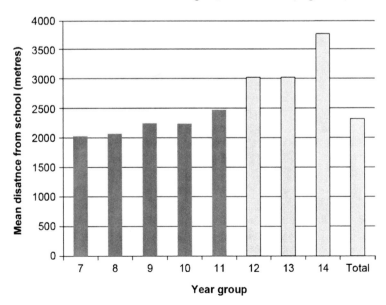

Figure 8.2. Mean distance of students' homes from the Academy.

Numbers overall had grown probably because the Academy set out to be a school that was inclusive and designed to meet the needs of the students there. The Principal said:

> It strives to genuinely help youngsters reach their potential, a student with a mountain of problems, like Peter, who would never be on the Health and Social Care course in the upper sixth with a chance of doing a degree if we'd run a traditional school with traditional values, whatever that means, and a traditional approach to relationships with students. This school is about students like Peter, which makes the whole thing much, much harder because some twit in central government has said that you have to get 30% A-C with English and maths and of course our current year 10 against Fisher Family Trust [calculations] tells us that we would be in the top 25% of schools if they got 8–9% with English and Maths and yet I am telling the staff we are going to make 25%.

Year after year results improved, shown graphically in Figure 8.3. Very respectable levels of 5A*-C results were achieved, close to the national average, attributable in part to the curriculum, purposefully designed for success through vocational courses.

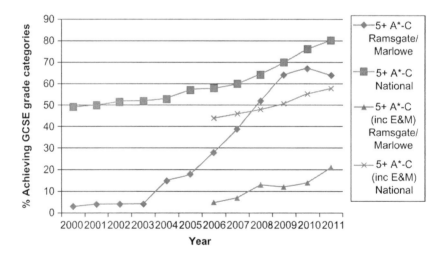

Figure 8.3. GCSE attainment levels nationally and at The Marlowe Academy.

While the rise in attainment levels had been remarkable, there were problems with maths and English. Mr J expected that maths would be up to 40% and assessments towards the end of the summer term 2011 indicated English at 30%, which would get them to the overall target of 25%. In the event it was 20%.

Attendance was a key contributor to success and, as Figure 8.4, shows, this improved to close to the national average attendance rate. Attendance at schools in extremely challenging circumstances is often something of a paradox, where non-attendance of some of the more challenging young people is met with relief. That was not the stance taken and everything was done to achieve high levels of attendance and maintain them. From an absence rate that was double the national average, and adversely commented on by HMI, the attendance rate rose to within two per cent of the national average.

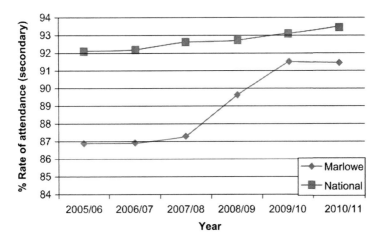

Figure 8.4. The Marlowe Academy and national secondary school attendance rates.

Exclusions provide another indicator of success of the inclusive intent of the Academy. The Ramsgate School had always been a very high excluder. The number of permanent exclusions at The Marlowe shows huge variability: over the most recent three years the numbers are eight, three, and eight – well above the national average rate. Fixed period exclusions rates in the most recent two years were 35% and 41%, four times the national average. Again, the pressures of striving for higher attainment levels in maths and English may have lowered tolerance levels and staff may have felt the need for more support in the exercise of discipline in class. Establishing the MAAC was in part a response to the judgment that too many were being excluded.

HOW THE ACADEMY WAS OFFICIALLY JUDGED

Ofsted reports gave another perspective on The Marlowe Academy. These were good for most of its six years of existence. The first inspection in June 2007 rated the 2006 achievement good, 'although well below national average standards, significantly higher than that achieved by the predecessor school and also much higher than expected given students' starting points.' It praised the extended day noting that 'its carefully orchestrated study group for each year group ensures that every student receives exceptionally good support'. It noted 'raised aspirations' and demonstrated that social circumstances are not an excuse for low ambition with 13 students expected to be moving on to higher education in the September.

The majority of students were well-behaved and 'the quality of learning matched the quality of teaching exactly' and the Academy was 'very well led [with] the drive to raise standards unrelenting'.

The March 2008 report had some criticisms like feedback on students' work frequently restricted to general comments like 'good work' and 'the integrated studies programme in Years 7 and 8 is not addressing students' literacy needs rapidly enough'. There is the suggestion that the leadership team, while adhering to the 'strong and distinctive ethos … did not give enough emphasis to the impact on students' achievement'. Though attendance at this time was still a problem, the overall Ofsted scoring of elements of the Academy contained more 2s (Good) than 3s (Broadly average). A monitoring visit in May 2009 reported very positively, referring back to results from the summer of 2008, noting that, 'Given the students' very low attainment on entry, the GCSE results in 2008 placed the Academy in the top 5% of schools for the progress students made when measured against their starting points'. However, the October 2010 inspection reported more negatively, giving the Academy an overall rating of 4 (inadequate) and a 'notice to improve … because it is performing significantly less well than in all the circumstances it could reasonably be expected to perform'.

The 'cohesive community' and pastoral support and guidance, had always been praised as was behaviour, but 'students make inadequate progress mainly because progress in English and mathematics is too slow.' Teaching was judged to be 'too variable in quality'. This was disappointing and, although the monitoring visit in May 2011 was positive, it was clear that much would rest on GCSE results in August 2011. At 20%, this was below what had been hoped for and it marked the end for an inspirational Principal before the start of the Autumn term 2011.

The sixth form was a very important part of The Marlowe provision, showing what was possible and how students could move on. It was praised in all the reports and the community spirit within the Academy was consistently labelled good. The sixth form was inclusive and in 2010 they were running a Level 2 course for those who were up to this point fairly low attainers – or just needed more time. The Academy sought to support them through to their next step. But that was not enough and the Principal said as much. The children attending The Marlowe were the same children of ten years before, yet now they were achieving better, going further and were in a more accepting and nurturing environment.

Mr J had himself taken over the running of English for the 2010–11 year and students entered with what was said to be the lowest scores at 11 of any mainstream secondary school in the country (possibly the lowest 3 or 5). It was accepted that results should be better but there were difficulties in recruiting good English and maths teachers and quality leadership in those subjects. The Academy was a year late getting on to the English and maths requirements because of staff weaknesses, key staff missing through illness or maternity leave and the Principal being sidetracked supporting two other academies, allowed perhaps because the trustees were so confident in the Academy's trajectory of results continuing.

Significant numbers went on to university, many supported by annual bursaries of £1,000 from the trust fund set up by Roger De Haan. It should be noted that university completion rates for these students were not high – 31% from the 2008/09 group though some had taken a year out and others were re-sitting exams. It is likely that students from these environments need more support, not just financial, to see them through the cultural shock higher education especially when it is away from home.

Table 8.3. Numbers of students going on to university and bursaries

Year	Total going to university	Bursaries	% receiving bursaries
2007/08	5	5	100%
2008/09	16	16	100%
2009/10	25	21	84%
2010/11	16	13	81%
2011/12	15	13	87%

REFLECTING ON SIX YEARS AS THE MARLOWE ACADEMY

As one member of staff said, Mr J could have raised the school's scores by recruiting more nice kids from favoured areas and was admired for not doing that. Noting the declined option, Mr J said,

> You can do it the hard way. Which is about trying to run as inclusive a school as possible that is designed and set up to meet the needs of the youngsters that you have. So you have your EBD and ASD and your EAL and your welfare and everything else. You have your breakfast clubs and all your staff having lunch alongside students. And you try a non-aggressive approach to managing student behaviour, non-confrontational, because you know that's what the youngsters are used to and they'll just rise to the bait and it'll be a war zone. We chose to develop an ethos based on emotional intelligence where the adults model how to be good adults. That is why I will not tolerate staff shouting at students, being aggressive and intimidating them because the kids would just copy it. That's what you do in a position of power.

The negative inspection report in the autumn of 2010, 'was a complete knock-back', 'a bombshell'; some teachers left, there was more pressure on people and they felt that they were going to be told they were useless again. The observation of lessons became more important and more worrying. If you got an unsatisfactory then you would be put on competence arrangements which could lead to dismissal.

The 14% in the Summer of 2010 was a disappointment and the observations system at the Academy and feedback arrangements were changed to mirror Ofsted requirements more closely. After the application of the new observation system, staff who six months earlier had been graded outstanding were down to satisfactory. They thought they had been doing everything right. There was a definite feeling of unfairness. The targets were unrealistic. They were told as a staff, from Mr J downwards, that they were not doing a good job. Teachers felt lost and undermined by the repetition in the report that leadership was fine, but a percentage of teachers were not.

In striving to comply with Ofsted requirements, the school felt it was becoming more regimented. Mr J acknowledged that the exciting teaching was disappearing under the weight of the new requirements. Recruitment and retention were affected.

Most frustrating, was the fact that many of the things that the Academy was doing well counted for nothing. So much effort was put in with individuals who made great progress, but not to the extent of reaching 5A*-Cs. The pressure on staff increased, as it did also on pupils. Fixed term exclusions increased. The knock on effect was that if you gave fixed term exclusions, the student then fell further behind. In maths, in 2011, 40% of students achieved grade A*-C but, as one maths teacher said, 'In order to achieve their higher grades, we bored them to death by exam practice'.

A school like The Marlowe was fragile. 'We were so close, so nearly there'. Having aspirations was virtually unheard of in The Ramsgate School. Behaviour was no different at The Marlowe though it was managed differently. It was not bad, as one teacher put it, 'It was just habitual'. It did not erupt. People were vigilant. Indeed, the Ofsted reports did not criticize the Academy for student behaviour.

A senior teacher said, 'I have learnt that you cannot afford to miss things, cannot take your eye off the ball. You have to keep reflecting on what you are doing and develop. We should have sustained the work with the community. The pressures the school faces are huge, not that I think it can't succeed. The system works against us. We are a successful school'.

The Marlowe had undoubtedly been transformational and was nothing like its predecessor school. The quite spectacular changes were in terms of:

- annual increases in student numbers
- high attendance levels achieved
- 5A*-C results at GCSE level
- sixth form and numbers going on to university
- huge reduction in those Not in Education Employment or Training (NEETs)
- the way the school community had become more cohesive
- sound partnerships with the LA and it agencies
- partnerships with police and voluntary sector.

Added to this, the fighting, the racism, the swearing at staff, the smoking had all dropped significantly. The extensive, positive support and guidance within the 'emotionally literate' ethos of good relationships and mature tolerance had much to do with these achievements. Children felt very safe, gay children were able to feel secure and students knew who to go to if they were troubled, upset or could not handle a lesson. The students knew the key person for them and that person would support them and work things out with them.

Most of all, and impressive to any visitor, was the faith in the young people's capacity to learn, the respect shown to them and the reluctance to point to problems in the young people's lives and community as justification for low performance. After 2009, the Academy had to compromise on some of its professed values and principles in order to reach government floor targets (35% 5A*-C GCSEs for 2012) while serving ALL students. Recruitment of quality experienced staff was an enduring problem. The big questions for the future, as Mr J assessed the situation, were:

a) managing the budget to maintain the 5pm finish time which has been so valuable in avoiding the homework problems and in developing the skills of independent learning
b) developing links with other secondary schools to share expertise, challenges and results
c) fair banding of students at secondary transfer so that there is a more equitable distribution of challenging students.

The Director had reflected on the particular challenge of improving those schools in the bottom 20% of the National Challenge[19] category i.e. the bottom 100 secondary schools in England. The same ingredients as for any school improvement initiative were needed – quality teaching, good governance, clear leadership, an appropriate curriculum, and raised aspirations. It is extremely difficult to bring all these ingredients together in such schools. Hence his conviction that community links and community revitalisation were both required. Learned optimism in the student body was also vital.

So much was positive, a remarkable social environment had been produced and the improvements in attainment were proceeding steadily. Whilst adjustments, some refocusing of teaching effort, tighter monitoring of learning and better academic focus for teaching assistants may have been called for, a dramatic change of leadership was arguably not necessary, yet axing heads not delivering up to the national benchmarks was the sort of action encouraged by recent governments. Mr J's big questions were reluctantly pointing to problems the Academy might not be equipped to address alone long term. Hence the reference to sharing expertise with neighbouring schools and a fairer distribution of challenging students.

Mr J's focus was seen as still strong in 2010/11 and he could still take tough decisions about staff who were not making it. The Academy had established a sense of purpose which was quite remarkable. The Marlowe experience over six years constituted a model of how to succeed with a secondary school in exceedingly challenging circumstances, but it was a finely balanced strategy, highly, and unjustly, vulnerable to external changes and requirements. On top of this, it could not survive and prosper confidently if families and communities were left, or kept, poor and their children compelled to grow up with multiple disadvantages. Poverty as the underlying problem is discussed to a limited extent in the next chapter and is central to the arguments of Chapter 11.

SCHOOL IMPROVEMENT MEASURES – ACADEMIC RESEARCH, PRACTICAL INTERVENTIONS, FAILING, SUCCEEDING

INTRODUCTION

The Ramsgate School was a struggling school for a long time. Once local financial management of schools and publicising results in league table form were introduced then the inequalities between schools increased. This was the situation The Ramsgate School faced from 1994. Always classed as a difficult school, it became more so once the marketisation of schools became more explicitly established, though it was always there in Thanet's eleven secondary schools. The hierarchy was steeper than in most areas with the three grammar schools at the top, followed in the pecking order by the religious foundation schools, the favoured high schools and then the one, sometimes two, at the bottom. Always, The Ramsgate school was at the very bottom.

This situation is not a natural phenomenon but one created and sustained by local and national policies. If it is the unintended consequence of these policies it is still recognised and accepted. It is considered collateral damage at best and what the undeserving poor have coming to them at worst. Poor schools giving a bad deal to local children and communities are avoidable if ruling elites and beneficiaries of the current systems accepted a share of responsibility for this injustice. Being born into a poor family where parents have little experience of educational success themselves should not mean greatly raised odds against the child being an educational achiever and getting employment, pay and general life chances that usually flow from this.

THE FORCES THAT DRIVE A SCHOOL DOWN

There has been a lot written about school effectiveness and school improvement. What causes school *in*effectiveness, or school deterioration even, is the mirror image question. The sorts of answers we get in the 21st century are very much 'of their time'. From the end of the second world war until 1990, your school was the one on your doorstep, or the grammar school to which you had 'won' a place; 168 grammar schools still exist in 2012 in 36 of England's 151 LAs. Kent has 33 of these grammar schools. Nor should we ignore the 7% of children whose parents pay for private education[20] and the privilege that seems to guarantee.

As described in Chapter 3, until around 1992, the Conyngham School was a decent, well-enough respected secondary modern doing its best for those in the local area, enjoying the public, untroubled secondary modern role and a certain private satisfaction amongst staff and pupils. You were what you were and you did what you did and that applied at institutional level as well as personal. There was not a great deal of comparing. Where there was comparison, it was certainly the case that from 1975 onwards the Conyngham/Ramsgate School was bottom of the heap. But it seemed a benign judgement and staff who went to teach at the school knew it was a tough assignment – but many were looking for just that. Teachers from those times talked in a way that conveyed the sense of pride and self-worth that comes from carrying through a difficult assignment well. Through it all, there is a sense of affection for the pupils and, at a minimum, an acceptance of the families.

The time since the mid-1990s has been an unfortunate, competitive, judgemental and blaming period. The causes of poor schools have not been considered in the context of *international comparisons* which take account of *poverty and its concentration*. The UK's *national policies,* the whole *local educational scene* which displaces blame from central and local government, and the operation of the sacred national *educational market* policies have all created a rationale for *blaming the victims*, with a knock-on motivation to *blame the teachers.* There is a *refusal to believe* that, if political will and financial redistributions are applied, *social engineering can lead to excellence* for all. In relation to schools 'failing', the rhetoric is about 'no excuses' and the exhortation of the coalition government of 2011 was for forcing up standards, not social engineering!

POVERTY, INEQUALITY AND LOW LEVELS OF ACHIEVEMENT

In all recognised international comparisons the UK does badly in both levels of inequality and the proportion of children growing up in poor families. The UK also comes out poorly by comparison with rich nations in terms of inequality in earnings. The Gini coefficient[21] is a comparison of the top 10% of earners and the bottom 10% and calculates by how much the bottom figure must be multiplied to equal the top figure. A greater proportion of people live in poverty in the UK and the UK's unemployment and other social benefits are less generous than those in other European countries. This means that welfare payments bring a smaller proportion out of poverty. More specifically, Figure 9.1 shows the United Kingdom compares poorly with European neighbours in terms of the proportion of children growing up in poverty defined as below 60% of the median family income. Mr Blair wanted child poverty eradicated by 2020, but the UK's child poverty programme is likely to fail; it has missed its targets for reduction year on year.[22] Yet poverty is so strongly related to achievement in schools that the greater the proportion of children growing up in poverty, the greater will be the number with low aspirations and low achievements.

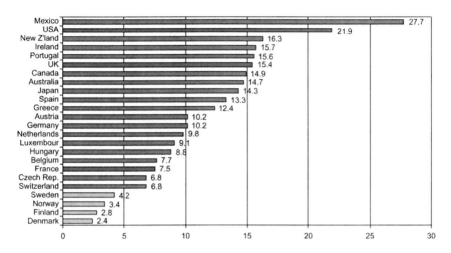

Figure 9.1. Percentage of children living in 'relative' poverty defined as households with income below 60% of the national median (UNICEF, 2005).

Within England, the association between attainment and poverty is so obvious and strong that 'closing the gap' goals have been pursued with some apparent energy. Yet it proceeds without attending to child and family poverty issues. Children from lower socio-economic groups are on average measurably behind at 22 months.[23] On entry to school, the gap is substantial as shown in Figure 9.2. On average, four out of ten children from the most deprived areas achieve a good level of development compared with six out of ten from the least deprived areas.

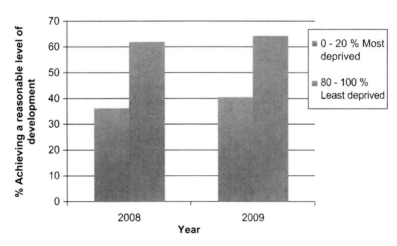

Figure 9.2. Percentage achieving a good level of development at the Foundation Stage (5 years old) England.

The picture is similar for children aged 11 with routinely lower proportions of children from poorer households achieving the expected levels in maths and English.

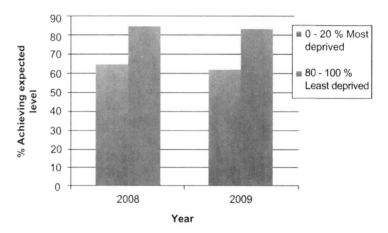

Figure 9.3. Percentages achieving the expected levels in English and mathematics at Key Stage 2 (11 year-olds) England.

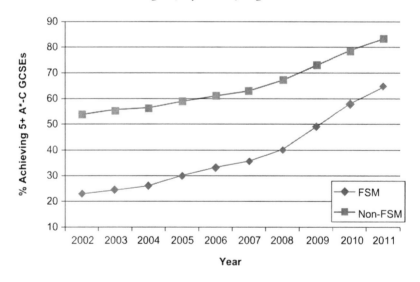

Figure 9.4. Percentage of pupils achieving 5+ A* to C GCSEs and equivalent by eligibility for Free School Meals 2002 to 20011 (16 Year-olds) England.

Figure 9.4 shows that the gap had closed over 10 years, possibly a result of the efforts and investment. In 2011, three out of five children eligible for free school meals (FSM) achieved five good GCSE passes compared with four out of five children who were from ineligible, better off families. It is important to note that the attainment gap is somewhat bigger when schools in the top 10% for FSM are compared with the 10% with lowest rates of FSM. For 5 A*-C grades including maths and English, the respective rates are 35.1% and 62.5%. Children attending a school whose intake is from poor communities are only half as likely to get 5A*-Cs including maths and English. The inclusion of maths and English as necessary elements in the calculation of standards from 2009 has hit hard those secondary schools which had designed a curriculum around vocational courses which earned four or more GCSE equivalents but did not include these two core subjects. So it was with the Marlowe Academy.

Looking at the two primary schools which serve the concentration of low earning and poor households from which the Marlowe drew some of its intake shows a very large difference, up to 2009, between the scores on Communication, Language and Literacy and Personal and Social Education for five year-olds and the average for Kent and England. A nationally funded project was part of the huge effort to raise the pre-school attainment but this ended in 2010 and scores have fallen for the two schools while continuing to rise for Kent and England as is evident from Figure 9.5.

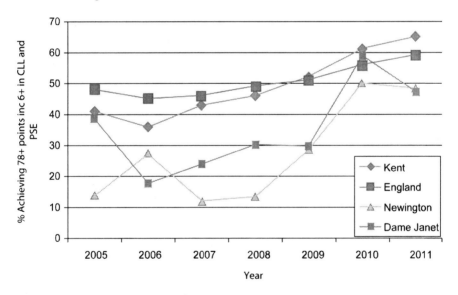

Figure 9.5. Percentage of children at the Foundation Stage (age 5) in two local schools compared with county and national levels of pre-school attainment.

Figures 9.6 and 9.7 show that, whereas the national average percentage attaining Level 4 in English was around 80%, for the Marlowe it had only recently risen to 50%. A similar picture emerged for maths.

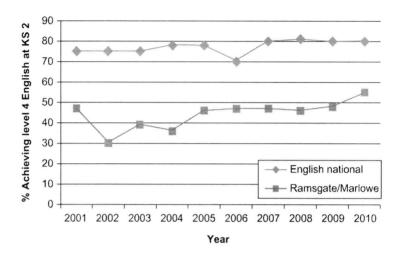

Figure 9.6. Percentage of children achieving the expected Level 4 in English at Key Stage 2 on entry to The Ramsgate School/Marlowe Academy.

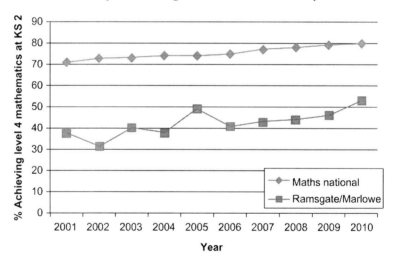

Figure 9.7. Percentage of children achieving the expected Level 4 in Mathematics at Key Stage 2 on entry to The Ramsgate School/Marlowe Academy.

Prior attainment remained doggedly fixed for neighbourhoods over years. Though locally improvements were achieved, the national levels rose too. The Marlowe's Contextual Value Added (CVA) up to KS 4, taking account of deprivation factors and levels of attainment at intake, had been largely good over the years. The investment and interventions needed at the youngest ages are huge and clearly insufficient is allocated at those stages. At 11, the children are behind and cannot but struggle with the increasingly demanding and complex educational challenges.

This is at a time of their lives when one might have hoped they would enjoy their learning, be equipped to engage with material and ideas with pleasurable vigour and ultimately achieve good certificated outcomes – almost as a by-product of enjoyable learning.

NATIONAL EDUCATIONAL MARKET POLICIES

When it comes to the ways schools perform, there are reasons (excuses?) for some coming bottom of the pile. Matters are so arranged that some schools must come bottom and the English way is to lampoon these, have documentaries to titillate viewers, and blame the victims. Easy.

Market competition in education has a lot to answer for; you drive a school down by comparing it unfairly, making it responsible for its budget and policies with little recognition of extra challenges and you cause staff disaffection and compromise recruitment by devaluing all that made the school function as an OK place as far as most of the parents and children in the neighbourhood were concerned. To publish secondary school results in league tables without taking account of the levels of attainment of children on entry to the school at 11 is unjust. Not to recognise the proportion of children from poor families, the proportion with special needs, the numbers of looked after children placed by social services and the numbers of asylum seekers and others whose first language is not English is plainly ridiculous. Naming and shaming is supposed to drive up standards, but how this is supposed to work is seldom explained by anything other than naïve assertions, and it is doubtful whether it works.[24] No government has commissioned evaluative studies to find out. The changes that came in with the National Curriculum and school league tables were divisive and corrosive – but it looks as though the way the major UK political parties have been thinking, we cannot pull back from them now.

The national arrangements for education are one major cause of decline. The idea that schools compete and the poorer ones try harder to get on a level with the better ones is absurd market competition thinking. Originally, it had been thought that, as parents exercised their rights to choose a school, the less popular ones would shrink and the better performing ones would expand. What *actually* happens is that schools choose! In Kent, the grammar schools select on the basis of test results, and the church schools select on the basis of religious affiliation. Many pupils cannot go to the school of their choice. An academically less successful school in an area will have spaces – and guess who goes there; but it still does not fill the school and casual admissions, and pupils excluded or squeezed out of other schools come to the one with places. The Ramsgate School was that school.

Unwillingness to admit the true situation leads to the temptation to *blame the pupils* and families from which they come for any low achievement. The blaming can seep into the very being of even well-meaning professionals when initial low achievement on entry to the school is regarded as reason enough to have low expectations, not try very determinedly in the teaching and just survive and get by.

BLAME THE TEACHERS

Then there is *blame the teachers*. The charge is that the teachers aren't good enough, don't try hard enough and are not committed. This is undoubtedly unfair on the large majority of teachers: some at The Ramsgate school were undoubtedly good. Some struggled but you could not be sure that they were to blame. However, some were clearly not up to the challenge. Often these were unqualified teaching staff, or teachers who were unable to get jobs at more highly esteemed schools. Both of these last two groups were often unsupported and the culture was very much one of in-at-the deep-end, gladiatorial challenge. A feature of The Ramsgate School staff culture in the late 90s was that middle management level teachers who had their own section in order kept it that way and were wary about expending energy outside their department. It led to bastions of order but no sense of whole school determination to hold the line.

Most of all, with so-called failing schools, it is claimed to be *a matter of leadership*: why else the faith in the 'super head'? Many examples exist in the media of heroic new head teachers 'turning a school around'. There are books and articles as well as more down-market magazine and local paper pieces on making a success of leadership of a school 'in challenging circumstances'. What is certainly not agreed upon is whether the best approach is to be tough on staff and pupils or to set clear expectations that are firmly applied while providing nurture and support. The Ramsgate School experienced the full range of these approaches over the five year period. None of the approaches prior to Ramsgate School closing and the Academy opening appeared to be, or were talked about, as drawing on any theoretical notions. There appeared to be little by way of explanation of low attainment and bad behaviour beyond finger pointing at the children, the families and the community. The team which took over from May 2003 must be excepted from this judgement. Fierce though their tactics were, they were committed to the view that the children deserved better and that poor teaching was at the root of the problem. For this, Mr H, in what was assuredly an oversimplification, publicly blamed previous leadership of the school and the local authority which allowed this to happen.

IMPROVING SCHOOLS IN CHALLENGING CIRCUMSTANCES

With all the above reasons for low attainment, low levels of engagement with education and poor behaviour, it is easy to understand cynicism and complacency in staff in such schools. The repeated finding from research that only up to 20%, no more, of the difference between schools' attainment is accounted for by what the school does is another dispiriting message. Yet despite logic, experience and evidence during Labour's years of investment and in the period of the coalition after 2010, national policy has been based on the aspiration and expectation that the attainment of these children will be improved by after-the-event intervention in the schools. 'Success against the odds' is what is sought. It may be only in politics that stupidity can pose as a moral commitment. Why should odds be stacked against some? Why should children grow up in disadvantage that they had no part in choosing or creating? Why does a nation not feel massive guilt at its lack of commitment to improving the lot of the very young being brought up in extremely challenging social circumstances? Why is there not more anger, more rioting, more bitterness from the populations at the receiving end?

To improve schools facing extremely challenging circumstances (SFECCs) is hugely difficult when tackled in the English way of limited intervention. Many books have been written about school improvement but few are convincing about those schools stuck year after year at the bottom. This partly explains why schools have been closed and reopened as new entities to allow restaffing and restyling. Academies in particular have taken steps to remove the most troublesome (and troubled) youngsters and attract children from more affluent areas. This was not a solution pursued by the Marlowe and indeed was considered inappropriate and improper if the school was going to focus on meeting the needs of the local population. The executive head in 2003 stated his position for making a bad school adequate – get the kids to behave and then teach them something. But among the school's intake at age 11 disadvantage was already present, so before long, the principal of the Academy was certainly coming round to the view that some fair distribution of children and cooperative working across schools was required; he had seen the problems of maintaining staff and balancing pressures on staff and students whilst retaining their commitment and durability.

The Director of Education had acknowledged the challenges of improving the worst 20% of the national challenge schools, probably 100+ secondary schools country-wide, and that this would involve community regeneration. Schools are not in the business of generating jobs in the local area, though in a very small way they do this with the employment of locals as teaching assistants. Regeneration of neighbourhoods has been tried, but this is usually tackled via limited term initiatives that seldom add up to a coordinated, long term campaign, let alone a national policy.

Improving a tough school takes energy, huge amounts of it. Mr J regularly worked 14 hour days and other staff at the Academy registered how they had to be present around the building throughout the day with relentless demands for attention and problem solving. Staff had to be constantly vigilant and 'could not afford to take your eye off the ball'. Mr H, five years earlier, and only half joking, stated that his two years in charge at The Ramsgate School had almost certainly shortened his life span. Earlier, Mr K lost two stone in weight. The leadership team has to be prepared to be energetic and ready to engage with the student body, parents and the community. They have to come across as confident and committed workers capable of exciting respect and confidence in others.

Improving a failing schools requires a team and this is not just a collection of individuals however talented they may be singly. Mr H understood that the previous head teachers had been lone operators and he, fortuitously, had a very talented team. This team was characterised by a common mission, signed up to the same ideals, an arm in arm phalanx which moved forward together and spoke with a single voice. If other teachers came to question what another of the team had instructed, they would get the same answer. It may have been an aggressive, militaristic, steely regime but the Academy's Mr J had an equally steely stance even if it played out differently.

From 2005, the senior leadership team of the Academy usually numbered more than 12 and it was not loyalty as such that Mr J sought, but a sign-up to the values and readiness to model the behaviour that went with these. In contrast to the 2003/04 rescue team, there was no shouting, no bells and tannoys and no 'punishment unit'. Exclusions were massively reduced, numbers grew again and attainment of 5A*-C grades rose from the 2005 level of 18% to 64% in 2009. The school was calm, twice-weekly assemblies showed the whole school to be a community that could work together and some growing confidence from the community was evident as more local children chose to attend the school. Nonetheless, at root there was the understanding that good learning came about from good teaching and teachers who were not making it at the Marlowe were moved on. This was done in a planned way. Good NQTs (Newly Qualified Teachers) were recruited early in the year for the September and huge efforts were put into professional development, monitoring, coaching and support. Mr J recognized that whilst pressure on both staff and students had its place, if you got it wrong the students could present more difficulties or staff could become demotivated. In these challenged circumstances, if there was criticism or bad publicity, morale could fall and recruitment could be more difficult; schools such as the Marlowe are not ones people are queuing up to teach in and, as one teacher said, he got some experience under his belt before coming to a school like this, which is where he ultimately wanted to be.

COLLECTIVE RESPONSE

The new Director found the county, in terms of local school structures, 'absolutely fragmented' and heads did not meet collectively. In Kent's mixed economy of schools, there were associations for heads of the grammar schools, church schools and high school but no shared ownership or sense of responsibility for the whole pupil population of the area. At public meetings he regularly shared his vision of a Kent where schools would collaborate and support each other and shared too his disappointment when this joint working fell short. And it did fall short in Thanet, however vocal headteachers were about supporting the weakest school. As Chapters 4 and 5 show, the other schools did not exert themselves to help The Ramsgate School. Support was still less in evidence once the Academy had opened. The LA had by some of its actions contributed to the failing position of the old school and other Thanet secondary schools benefited from a school with space to accept 'unwanted pupils, 'though it had knock-on problems as we all know', as one education officer said.

A senior teacher at the school said in 2011:

The school is in such a vulnerable position that you have to be good at everything. A school in a more advantaged situation could have a weakness here and there and would be fine. We do not fit into the expected framework for achievement. Some of our youngsters go on to year 12 and get their grades there. There are progression routes. The Academy had a certificate one year to say they were one of the most improved schools in the country. Then the criteria were changed and they were failing. It is arbitrary, farcical.

No one would want the school to be one praised for its pastoral system, for the pleasant atmosphere and the child safeguarding if the learning is below accredited targets.

The Marlowe Academy received the Homes and Communities Agency *Community Award* in 2009 and figured as a DCSF Case Study published in 2010. It is a secondary school and sixth form with a dual specialism in performing arts and business enterprise. It has redefined its place in the local community, providing a shining example for other schools for its inclusiveness. The Academy's slogan is 'Proud to be different' and is a true reflection of the innovative measures that have been introduced since the Marlowe Academy opened.

It has a longer day starting at 8.30am and finishing at 5pm, with just short breaks between two-hour classes, no school bells and no homework! Mr J summed up the core of the Academy as:

> The longer day is all about supporting youngsters who probably wouldn't do their homework, kids who may not have their own computer or somebody willing or able to help or encourage them off site. Finishing any earlier is education by compromise. This is a buzzy, "can-do" school which celebrates the individual and their differences. To tackle attendance you need to create an environment that the students want to be in. The other side of it is chasing those that aren't attending to find out and address the reasons why. We don't run sin bins and we don't have withdrawal. Instead we have specialist teams who provide support to students who may need it.'

The vulnerabilities cannot be overlooked. A challenging school, a school facing challenging circumstances, a school with challenging children and a school where the prior attainments and the attitudes to education are poor is exposed to failure in many ways. Even if the curriculum plan by which the students are to learn is sound, the teacher student relationships are right, and the leadership is smart and strong, staffing is difficult. Running a senior management team capable of overseeing the various faculties and sections of the school is particularly subject to disruption if there is illness, departure of a key person or for one area the right candidates cannot be found. For the Marlowe, out on the parson's nose of Kent the catchment area for teachers is limited, unlike in a big city. A school like the Marlowe is vulnerable in relation to reputation and confidence, shaken it has to be said, by the change in league table criteria which put it in the bottom six in the country in 2011 with its 20% relevant grade attainment. Students are affected by news of its standing, parents more so. Teachers are less attracted to a school which is obviously such a struggle. There are only so many 'nutters', as Mr J put it, you can get into the school and if morale drops through public sneering, even the most upbeat, optimistic leader can lose the team spirit and commitment so necessary to sustain the stability and ethos of the school. A number of staff expressed a certain joy at working there but would acknowledge that it was taking a toll. Some wondered how long they could sustain their energy and commitment. Resources were clearly an issue but if this is for additional teachers in the core subjects, there remains the issue of actually recruiting them, since even offering enhanced pay has failed to attract a good field.

A SUCCESSFUL MODEL FOR IMPROVING A SCHOOL IN CHALLENGING CIRCUMSTANCES

In 2009, the Marlowe Academy was a success, moving forward, with numbers increasing year by year and KS 4 examination passes hitting an all time high. It is difficult to see how a 'driving up standards'/'no excuses' agenda helps a school like The Marlowe'. This was a pleasant school to be in, as most visitors would attest, probably even HMI who put the school in the category of *serious weaknesses*. The school was a well-regulated, safe place for children and they were learning. Fifty per cent special needs, free school meal entitlement at more than twice the national average and grown to twice the size of The Ramsgate School at the time of its closure, and still it was able to achieve these results.

The Academy reached a point where 15 students were expected to go to university in September 2011 and the Academy's NEETs (not in education employment or training) were below 2%, a huge reduction on previous years. The benchmarked standards, and particularly the changes in them and the whole national challenge policy posed problems for any school in the position of the Marlowe. The Academy had come so far yet was always, and in more recent years increasingly, vulnerable to external judgements. Negative publicity directly affected pupils and the staff who might be tempted to move. Indirectly, it made recruitment more difficult. Amazingly punitive sets of forces are faced by institutions at this level in the system. It is no great surprise if governing bodies or trustees are overpowered by the external judgements of Ofsted and the publicly available league tables showing comparable levels of achievement in the 5A*-C grades including maths and English and persuaded to change the school leader. The reversal of HMI and Ofsted judgements was hugely paradoxical when the school was judged to be in the top 5% in terms of value-added in 2008, was a DCSF case study school in 2010 and the upward trajectory in attainment was continuing. The model was working and could have worked better and quicker with a network of support from local schools and with a more radical strategy for education and care across the Newington estate. If families were taken out of poverty, the struggle would not be so great and the odds not so stacked against.

A SCHOOL TO SERVE: YOUNG PEOPLE AND PARENTS WITH VIEWS, HOPES AND ASPIRATIONS

INTRODUCTION

Young people want to learn. They learn from birth onwards and even elderly adults can attest to the new learning that takes place into later life. Schooling is a particular sort of learning and school a very particular place for it to happen. There is also a particular set of materials and methods of learning there and relationships which can take many different forms. The home and the family are the more natural and more influential environments.

Parents love their children, want the best for them, are the most suitable carers, the ones with whom the children become comfortable, from whom they learn most and for whom the greatest loyalties are felt. The exceptions to this are small in number and usually associated with drugs, alcohol, extreme criminality, mental health problems or learning difficulties. The proportion of looked after children[25] (children fostered or otherwise in the care of the local authority) is very small (65,000) out of a population of young people in England aged 0–16 that stood at the 2001 census at 11 million. Over a third of the children in public care are in the compulsory secondary school age range and the outcomes, when the state takes over are, in general terms, woeful. Parents are the best hope for most children for their progress educationally, emotionally, physically and for their future life chances. The parents may well be part of an extended family network which offers additional support and sponsorship of the children.

This chapter is about listening to some of the young people and their refreshing, often forthright, sometimes contradictory but always insightful observations of their situations. Adults know best is not always correct and we can see inconsistencies and contradictions amongst adults working in, running or making policy for the country's schools. Negotiation and listening are activities one would hope would prevail in schools and one might consider whether it is *relationship* policies that are needed rather than *behaviour* or *discipline* policies. The leadership in a school may be measured in some communities by how loud and repressive it is. But leadership can be equally steely whilst being supportive and moderate with a modelling of behaviour that remains consistent and respectful at all times. That is what Mr J's Marlowe Academy promised, and for the most part delivered. This is not to say that there was not admiration from some quarters for the resolute toughness of Mr H's regime in the two years before.

ASPIRATIONS OF YOUNG PEOPLE

Young people have ideas about where they want to go and what they want to do. It was evident that the 'can-do' atmosphere at The Marlowe Academy gave young people the idea that they had real choices about future careers, some quite ambitious but not ridiculously so. Some wanted to go to university and had the example of the many that had already made it – and come back to talk about 'life at uni'. Others were going into tourism or nursing or health and beauty, or 'something in the arts world'. They were in an environment where they all mattered and were respected and were given every encouragement to see a future for themselves.

The number going to university each year peaked at 25 in September 2009 and the proportion of students registered as NEETs was very low in 2010 and 2011. The Academy's aim was very much to be inclusive, to make students *want* to be. With absenteeism well down and close to the national average, part of that had been achieved. As one student said about the prospect of changes, 'It's good already. They'd have to be careful about changing things or you might get people dropping out.'

Some did not achieve because family issues and caring responsibilities got in the way and there could be resentment amongst those who did not get required grades at BTEC or GCSE. Sometimes a sense was conveyed that the school had let them down or they did not realise you had to work hard all through the year.

RELATIONSHIPS

Students described the school as 'laid-back', some adding 'perhaps too much so'. Their comments differentiated between how relations worked out in core subject lessons, compared with their vocational option area and generally around the school.

> There is this problem that because there is this focus on grades, we don't get the in-depth learning we need to retain the information. It's all well and good and looks good on paper and looks like we are making progress but because we have not had the detailed teaching we are failing in our exams. They are just trying to get the grades out of us.

A Year 10 student described how, earlier in the year, he was disciplined because he pointed out a way of running the class where it might be more effective. 'I actually took the teacher aside and suggested another way of doing things'. Another student remarked that, 'The teacher probably found that a bit patronising'. The first student went on to explain that he had gone higher up in the school with the head of department and then the head teacher, after expressing his personal concerns to the teacher, because nothing was getting done.

> It got to the point that I made a remark at the end of a lesson, it was not particularly spiteful, it was another suggestion, but it was in front of the whole class and I was told I was not welcome in that class and was banned for a series of lessons in that subject. That's a problem that the Marlowe faces – too set in its ways to listen to the students' concerns. Some will listen but it is in the core subjects where they won't.

This view was widely shared and this was in a school which prided itself on its calm, listening relationships with students.

> In the core subjects mostly, because all they want is the grades, they don't want to listen to the pupils because they want to do what they think is best. Because they won't listen to the pupils they don't know what is best. Without our input they don't know what is best, which means they are driving us through for the exam which means that we are not retaining enough information for the exam in the first place. They say this is the question, this is how you answer this question but then you don't know how to apply it to other questions of that type. If you say you don't understand, the teacher says, you weren't listening but I am listening and I don't understand and I need to get some help.

Being treated like adults applied less in these core lessons than around the school. Another student took this further:

> Some teachers will take you aside at the end of the lesson while others will 'degrade' you quite a lot by saying it in front of the whole class. When you say you don't understand and are told you were not listening, then other students turn round and say, 'Well I don't understand it either', and the teacher will go off in a massive fit.

As some saw it, a student could get into trouble by making constructive suggestions. 'If a student points out an injustice, the teacher will just say, "Don't argue with me. Don't tell me how to do my job. Just get on with it"'. The need to be taken seriously in core subject lessons was illustrated by the comment, 'Learning works both ways. The student needs to listen but needs to get involved as well'.

One can see the raised pressure to which Mr J referred when English and maths A*-C grades were to be included in the 5A*-C criterion. He acknowledged that this led to less tolerance, more fixed period exclusions and the need to balance supporting teachers against listening to students. With this pressure, it is easy to see how a divide can develop. Students recognised this and could see the purpose of the extra lessons in core subjects to prepare them for exams, but it meant being taken out of lessons for the extra inputs. So for maths they may be taken out of their art but that was their vocational option area and they wanted to do well in that too. One student noted that it had put him behind.

PRESSURE

Some students suggested that the pressure was not so great in the lower years and the students there had more help. Some could compare with their experiences in other schools they had attended where the pressure was considerable from Year 7. On the one hand, that was hard from the beginning, but they were used to it by the time the Key Stage 4 examination curricula were the priority. One student thought, 'It could be that it is so lackadaisical for so long that is the difficulty', while another said, 'For me there is not enough challenge, pressure and I would have liked that earlier on. Then it just comes like a smack in the face'. It seemed to be the view that, once in Year 11, they became subject to very short deadlines and high expectations. It became a very steep incline and if they had had some pressure earlier they think they would not have had these problems in Year 11. These are perceptions, energetically contributed, but it is as well to remember the caution of the younger student earlier about being careful when considering changing things, which might make it worse.

In the vocational subjects, relationships were reportedly better and teachers would listen. It has to be borne in mind that students choose their vocational option and spend overall more time with that teaching team. These four vocational areas had been the centre of the learning provision from the outset to meet the perceived educational needs, attributes and aspirations of the young people. This curriculum arrangement was also judged to be the best one to meet the 5A*-C criterion with these students, in this school and in this community. One Year 11 student described with great confidence and approval the work they did on the Health and Social Care course.

> There are nine units and the first one is *Communication* and we have to learn
> about how to communicate with elderly people, because elderly people have
> a view of teenagers and think they are trouble makers and stuff and we went
> to the Age Concern centre for an hour a week.

Twenty five students went and there was obvious approval for the way this element of the course responded to and developed their talents. The elderly people were invited for Christmas lunch in what was quite obviously a mutually rewarding experience. Most striking was the confident way the student spoke of the course and its components conveying a sense of it belonging to and making sense to her. Without wanting to take this too far, more abstract and academic subjects just do not do that for some students in their teens.

There was some erosion of these courses and their central place in the Academy's curriculum offerings. National governments, Labour in 2008, and the coalition government from May 2009, considered the vocational route to five good GCSEs to be 'a bit of a fiddle' and made the additional demands of the five good passes having to include maths and English. Bearing in mind the quite astonishing rise in five A*-C grades to 64% by 2009 (see Table 7.1), it was perverse to bring in such a hurdle. As Mr J had remarked, the National Challenge Strategy of pressure to improve by ever narrower criteria could 'derail a school like the Marlowe'.

Circulating around the Academy confirmed what students said, 'We are treated like adults in the sense that we are treated with respect, they listen to us, they talk to us.' More than that, there were opportunities for students to get help to sort out their problems, 'If you come in upset you can go into the welfare office and you can talk about it'. The staffing of the welfare office and the queues that had once formed testified to the need for and popularity of their work.

One girl came to the Marlowe from another secondary schools because she was bullied. Then, the girl who had bullied her came to the Marlowe on a fresh start move. Mr J was alerted to the difficulty and, 'pulled us both out of lessons and took us to his office and sorted stuff out. It was sorted but I found that hard to do. I don't talk to her. I keep my distance. The school is good; if you have a problem there's always someone you can talk to'.

Two students mentioned that with these close relations there can be a 'trust problem' and one can imagine some disclosures which, for legal reasons, may have to be taken further. Over all, students appreciated that teachers were accessible in the open area and could be confided in, and that there were no nooks and crannies where bullying, smoking and other nefarious things could go on.

The openness of the school was something most were proud of, proud that any student could come to the Marlowe Academy and that people could come in from the community. The veterans' day, with a meal and entertainment for the old soldiers, was a special treat for both students and the vets. There have been huge efforts to establish a non-aggressive approach, from staff towards students and also between students. This has also involved addressing sexism, racism and homophobia. The Marlowe Academy World Awareness Day (MAWAD), which had been an annual event to contribute to multicultural awareness, was highly regarded. Students could recall the foods teachers from different countries had made and displayed on stalls and the dances and performances put on by students from different ethnic groups.

This openness extended to police officers and residents coming in. Students had no recall of anyone from the Innovation Centre coming in for lunch – but then they might not have recognised them. The open atrium area always seemed to be buzzing with staff groups sorting things out and some staff meeting visitors there. At all times there appeared to be the modelling of reasonable and polite adult interactions, and a similar style practised by teachers with students. And student-to-student interactions were for the most part congenial.

DISCIPLINE

Discipline troubled the students in that they felt the discipline procedures, displayed in colour in every classroom, were not consistently adhered to. A third warning was supposed to trigger a call to senior management but some teachers, the students said, gave warning after warning. Some students felt that those presenting discipline problems were given too many chances. As they saw it: 'The majority of the problem is with individuals and the self-control of particular students', but it was also recognised that there were some students that teachers did not have the patience for, not through any fault of the student, and that affected their learning. One student, regularly on the receiving end of disciplinary interventions, judged that it was too easy for teachers to throw a student out of class, 'They can get away with it. They are not doing their job!'.

Adolescence is a time of turmoil, energy and distraction. That is the teenager condition. Many would not want to quell the energy and the example of the two girls arguing vigorously about Jordan (Katie Price) in Chapter 8 was, in some ways, healthy. That it would not cease in the face of adult authority, is also a commonly reported feature of the behaviour of these mid-teen years. The Marlowe approach had never been to crush this but to tackle it with waves of intervention, some would say remorselessly applied, to get students to better understand what they had done and the effect on their learning and that of others. This may account for the less than consistent application of the disciplinary policy, and the apparently more lackadaisical atmosphere. This was a school which wanted pupils to *want* to attend, and which advocated resourcing lessons so that they had an element of entertainment and youth appeal, on the back of which learning and development could take place. It is important to bear in mind that, by all sorts of measures, it was the same kind of pupils attending in 2011 as in 2001. But in 2011 there were many more of them. For several years earlier in the decade, the school was worryingly unsettled and, some would say, unsafe. Certainly school attendance, actually being in lessons when in school, relationships and learning were all very bad. This had all changed.

The Marlowe Academy was still a school facing extremely challenging circumstances with high percentages of students with special needs and free school meal entitlement and a proportion who would not otherwise be in mainstream education. With the chosen policy to have no punishment (inclusion? exclusion?) unit and to support pupils in classrooms wherever possible, a special tolerance of all students was required.

Approaches to discipline can reveal a cultural divide. There was almost universal agreement amongst one group of mothers interviewed that the legal change ending of corporal punishment was a bad thing. One even went to the school and gave her own child a slap. The teacher said, 'You can't do that', to which she replied, 'He's my son. What are you going to do?' Discipline at the Marlowe was not regarded as good by these parents. Parents often expected a harshness, which the school would want to stand firm against while demonstrating that good order prevailed.

Given all the improvements achieved and the position The Marlowe Academy had reached, one may almost suspect a conspiracy to see the achievements of its students, and those in all other schools in similarly challenging circumstances, so undermined by a capricious change to a major criterion of success. However, the change appears to have been made without reasonable consultation, and probably for political reasons of presentation. All too often such political changes are irresponsible. Experienced professionals, if consulted, could have easily foreseen the consequences for SFECCs that followed. Even if a political decision was made to accept this collateral damage, it reinforces the perception that government policy too readily ignores the plight of those sections of the population in severely challenging circumstance. As one sixth form student remarked to the local press in June 2011, 'It's annoying when people say you go to a rubbish school. I've done really well here, but the trouble is, once a school gets a bad reputation, it tends to stick.' In 2012, she was at university pursuing a degree course, one of 16 who went on to university, most of whom had started their secondary education at The Ramsgate School and continued through the Marlowe years.

HOMEWORK AND THE EXTENDED DAY

There were universal moans from students about the long days and the study periods in which to do homework. Although this latter system was explicitly designed to avoid the problem of homework not being done, so often the case in schools with children from poorer families, the students would have liked the choice about whether to do homework at school or home, 'so that you can do it in your own time and own pace'. They talked very sensibly about what to do if people did not do their homework. 'If they don't do it at home, then they should have to stay at school to do it before being allowed another attempt to do it at home.' They thought a homework club would be best.

STUDENTS WITH ATTITUDE

The students I interviewed or less formally chatted with were assertive and shared their opinions eagerly. These were students from much the same backgrounds as those who, 10 years before, had been virtually running riot in the school. They now displayed the optimism which the Director had hoped academies would foster and which the Principal held as a key goal. Even when there had been disputes and dissatisfaction with the regime, the students expressed their views as though within an inclusive community, not as a resentful, oppressed, suppressed set of outsiders with little hope.

THE CAPABILITIES AND HOPES OF PARENTS

They are a number of dimensions which affect the power and effectiveness of parents, some of which are not within their power to determine. The more immediate dimensions are: their learned capacity as parents; preparedness to engage with education; and how to relate effectively with interventions designed to support families. More distant from the local context are: initiatives to close the gap(s) between poorer families and others; the national context for engaging, supporting and intervening with children and families in challenging circumstances; and getting out of poverty. These issues structure the rest of this chapter. What follows is informed by understandings of the role of parents in education in England and related to the reported experiences of the Marlowe parents.

THE CAPACITY OF PARENTS

Parents with limited educational background and little success at school are restricted in their ability to guide their children with their school work and behaviour when at school. Often, parents have negative memories of school and report discomfort on entering a secondary school as adults. Added to this, there can be some negative attitudes towards study and difficulties providing appropriate behavioural advice and example rather than emphasising 'sticking up for yourself' and not taking insults from anyone. When such parents go to the school to complain, it can be a loud and conflict-prone experience for the school staff they encounter.

In the same way that children vary in their attitudes to and interactions with the education system, parents show a similar range of responses. Only one third of the pupils are from homes which are financially poor, as indicated by free school meals entitlement, and some of the families know what educational success looks like. They can provide the means to achieve it in the home: knowledgeable involvement with school work, discipline, examples of reading for extended periods, discussion or at least argument using evidence, and tolerance of different values. Other, more general, parenting skills are extremely valuable. If children can be helped to plan ahead, appreciate the consequences of their actions, and adapt their behaviour to different social settings, they will be well placed to learn co-operatively, and live and work successfully with just about anyone.

For some children, such as Pat's in Chapter 2, one envisages the two daughters being supported extensively in their education, and Pat herself was involved in junior school education. Sometimes there are issues of space to do homework, even if take-home homework was minimal from the Marlowe. Suitable space is needed for quiet, studious activities, which might involve reading, or sustained attention to a hobby. There are also matters of encouragement and aspiration. As one parent put it, 'If they don't want to learn, they won't. I have always pushed my kids. No one could say I haven't, but if they don't want to, well, you can only do as much as the kid will allow'. The 'pushing' may not always be in tune with what is best for school progress.

Firm boundaries and consistent discipline are always appropriate in the home and usually in line with what is encouraged at school, although some parents favoured harsher treatment for bad behaviour, and thought discipline at the Marlowe to be 'soft'. However, the biggest handicap in the educational progress of Marlowe students was the low literacy levels with which they entered secondary school and the lack of exposure to and encouragement for reading they had at home. Reading novels and regular perusal of newspapers was reportedly limited. This latter situation prompted Mr J to devote one of his weekly assemblies to news items, as recounted in Chapter 8.

Progression on to higher education for one time Ramsgate School pupils had happened in earlier decades and teachers from that time gave accounts of those singular successes, usually happening well into adulthood – as was the case with Pat's daughters. The Marlowe, by establishing the sixth form, and Mr De Haan, by providing bursaries, wanted to highlight the possibility of progression to the higher levels of learning and accreditation which provide access to professional jobs, pay and life chances. The twenty plus students going from the Marlowe to university in the best years should have challenged low aspirations, but whether the stories of this elevation were celebrated and disseminated energetically enough is not clear.

ENGAGEMENT WITH PARENTS

Schools have a duty to relate to the parents of their students and to develop cooperative relationships to support the child. Parents should not simply hand their children over to the school. There needs to be a continuing access for parents, and an encouragement to come into the school that is not limited to invitations to school events. This access should include opportunities to talk to senior staff and, in the case of the Marlowe, Mr J gave every parent his mobile phone number. Whether parents made contact in a reasonable and diplomatic way, or with aggression and raised voices, Mr C said, 'We will meet the parents wherever they are … even if they sometimes expressed it [their problem] in ways which were not easy to deal with' (Chapter 6). In Mr J's first year as Principal in the old Ramsgate School building he reported parents coming in and shouting at him.

It is important that key staff are confident enough, well-disposed towards parents, and willing to listen to, and understand, the issues raised by them. The best outcome for potential disputes is an agreement between the school and the parents that they will together address the problem, agree a joint strategy and keep in contact about progress.

A school's reputation is built over years and one like the Marlowe has to battle against a history of let-down and entrenched negative beliefs about what the local school could do for children. One Newington parent wanted her child anywhere but at the Marlowe (2011) and was relieved to get her first choice not too far distant. Another moved her daughter from the Marlowe to another school where she reportedly flourished.

One had to drag her partner to see The Marlowe Academy in its new building but even that did not change his mind. He agreed it looked good if you wanted to do performing arts. Another father did not bother to go to the open evenings for parents of Year 6 children and there was the often-heard remark that, 'It doesn't matter how much you knock it down and rebuild it, it will still be the same.'

However, there were parents vociferous in their support for the new Academy, even confronting negative talk about it in the gym and pubs, challenging people to go and see for themselves and giving their own evidence of successful work with their children. How extensive that support became is difficult to judge and the renewed reports of low attainment (on the revised national criterion) were a huge obstacle to generating admiration and acceptance.

One mother reported that, at the Marlowe, 'They do unbelievable things'. One had a son who got a job at the Marlowe (technician or teaching assistant) and 'loved it'. One had a daughter who did really well there and stayed on to the 6th form. Her other, more troubled, daughter had greater needs and the mother described how, 'If she did not turn up or there was an exam she had to be there for, the school would ring and sometimes get to speak to the daughter', with the implication that this would sometimes have the desired effect. The utterances that supported the school were generally more softly expressed than the critical ones: of teachers, one mother said, 'They have always been there to help me'.

It is amusing to hear the not altogether joke response to the question, what does the Marlowe Academy need? 'Sack all the teachers and get the parents in'. It displays a simplified view of education, of how easy it is to provide and what the ingredients of good teaching might look like, that is far from what is generally understood amongst professionals. Whether this is challenged in the most benign ways of getting parents in to observe school life, by sharing more explicitly 'the way we do things' with lesson examples placed on the web, or the more direct rebuttals of the student welfare officer as described in Chapter 8, is a matter of choice and resources. It is another feature of schools in challenging circumstances that, with all else that they have to do, self-promotion and marketing would also seem essential.

INTERVENTIONS WITH FAMILIES

Until secondary schools become full service community schools there will be limits to what a school can do by way of outreach to families. The Marlowe has achieved some elements of this and has also hosted on site counsellors, speech therapists and trainee social workers. Their impact has reportedly been good but these 'additional' services are highly vulnerable to funding cuts. The services are not considered central to the school's functioning by educators in England, though many would argue that learning cannot take place if other needs are not first met[26]. Mrs F relayed how she was shocked at the number of child protection cases she had to deal with, more than in any other school she had worked in over long experience. It is misleading to give excessive space to the 50% of children on the special needs register or the large minority of children from poorer homes, but this constantly stands at more than twice the national average. Nearly half the Marlowe students do *not* have special needs, two thirds are *not* from families with really pressing financial difficulties and 50% *had reached* the benchmark levels in English and maths at age 11 (Figures 8.6 and 8.7). Very few are looked after, refugee or transient even though these groups are present in higher proportions than in other Thanet schools. Essentially, with nearly half the students, the explicit markers of need for interventions are absent. The Marlowe celebrates and expects 'normality', expects all to prosper and promotes and celebrates the achievements of all kinds especially in assemblies and displays. It presents its school as one where the children of all families can succeed.

However, by comparison with other secondary schools in Thanet, there are additional needs in The Marlowe Academy and *some* services to address these. The student welfare office has workers who are local, born into the local scene, committed to the local area and long-term employees of The Ramsgate School and then the Marlowe. The welcoming, 'Come in darlin', sit yourself down for a moment, angel', 'How can I help you sweetheart', represents the non-judgemental, supportive style, often heard at the local supermarket check-out. While not quite how Ellie (Chapter 2) described the family liaison officer, 'She's been where I've been', these were not distant professionals. It is those non-punitive, befriending, but still expert, services that are needed with the sense that those employed are 'of us' and 'for us'. These people will act professionally to help parents make the best of their talents in providing support for their own children. The statutory and enforcement agencies, let us say social services and police, have their place and child protection (CP) and children in need (ChIN) processes are still there for the worst situations. It is a fact that poverty is more likely to produce conditions where drug and alcohol misuse occur, where mental health issues are more common and where criminality might flourish (see Chapter 1). Preventative services, if sufficiently robust and supportive, and available up to and beyond the age of 16, could do much to intervene in problems and insulate a child from the worst excesses. For some families there are crises and these pass; for others intervention needs to provide maintenance over the medium or long term.

In all this, although they are by no means 'well off', it must be stated that poverty is not the defining feature of the communities and the families that send their children to the Marlowe. As several adults I spoke to said (see Chapter 2), terms like 'poor', 'dysfunctional' and 'having no aspirations' were insulting and demonstrate a misunderstanding of the estate and its people. Sure Start children's centres fulfil the befriending *of us, for us and amongst us* service for some. Community involvement workers (CIWs) and health visitors associated with Sure Start can do some of the befriending and supporting. Community Wardens and Police Community Support Officers can also operate in a way which is non-threatening – even if strength and force are admired by some and PCSOs are referred to unkindly as 'wannabees'. Some Sure Start initiatives have extended their age range beyond four-year-olds and responded to needs of older children. The point is that early inoculation seldom works in the long term[27] without an adequate, sustained follow-through, possibly even to the extent of mentoring the peak successes through university and into work. This is not such a radical idea but simply an extension of support to ensure that earlier investment is not lost. The Sure Start children's centre in Newington had its money cut in 2011, the two Community Wardens who once just served Newington now have to spread their services across all the towns of Thanet, and the two PCSOs located in the temporary building to the south of the Newington estate, close to the children's centre, and Ms S, based in the Marlowe, cannot be regarded as having secure positions in times of cuts. These are vital preventative workers who, as it is, are not accessible or accessed by all, and their reach has been reduced. Cuts in such 'soft' services, which can struggle to show their utility in short term economic pay-offs, will reduce inclusionary efforts.

CLOSING THE ATTAINMENT GAP(S) WITH FAMILIES

The gap between the poorer students in a school and those from more affluent families endures. Correspondingly, students at secondary (and primary) schools from poorer households in aggregate lag behind those from better off households. Children from poorer families *on average* achieve lower grades than their better off peers, and are *more likely* to be excluded on a fixed term or permanent basis, to be on part-time timetables, or to be in alternative provision. Underachievement and poor behaviour start early. Today this is observable and measurable from two years of age onward – some researchers claim from even earlier[28]. These are not absolutes – being born poor does not condemn every child to relative failure – but *the likelihood*, confirmed by regularly recorded statistics, is remorseless, year on year. There is a timescale from birth to school leaving age and beyond that needs in-depth consideration by policy makers and lead practitioners when making decisions about sequencing interventions across this early life span. Unconnected, short term, age related initiatives are not enough, whether to address problematic behaviour or raise reading levels.

Children arrive at secondary school with six years of schooling behind them and most will have had some pre-school experience. It is important, if early intervention is to mean anything, that those children who have difficulty developing their basic skills, particularly literacy skills, are identified early and extra help is supplied. If a physical and emotional environment that fosters a reasonable development of the children is not present, then community or professional family improvement initiatives need to be generated. If challenging and anti-social behaviour is the problem (known broadly as Social, Emotional and Behaviour Difficulties – SEBD), then support for the child and the family to deal with this needs to be available and effectively applied.

The Marlowe's youth worker, PCSO, counsellor, speech and language therapist, the legion of teaching assistants and advanced level teaching assistants, the ASD base and the EDB unit as well as the student welfare and family liaison office constitute a richness of provision that goes significantly beyond what most secondary schools can offer. Section 52 funding returns show that the Marlowe received extra funding in recognition of the unusually high levels of social deprivation and of special needs among its pupils. However, the level of extra funding for schools with the biggest challenges is not enough when there are 900 students and significant numbers are 'in need' or 'at risk'. More resources are needed for such schools to offer as standard such services as social work, parent support, youth work, homework clubs and healthcare.

One can identify the extra expenditure that goes into those geographical areas labelled as deprived and it can appear significant. But the funding goes mostly to paying the salaries of middle class professional workers. It does not go into the family budgets of poorer families. Furthermore, the funding, which is too little by any calculation and at lower levels than most European countries, is spent to address the consequences of social and economic deprivation and not to reduce the poverty itself.

It is unrealistic to expect schools in these exceptional circumstances to achieve on a par with those in leafy, owner-occupied suburbs, or those that are assured of always having an intake that includes the top 30% of children by their tested ability at 11 years of age. It is ludicrous, defies logic and raises questions of competence of ministers and their civil servants, if the same expectations are applied with punitive axing of heads being the response to shortfalls. At the very least, these schools could be given more time to raise attainment levels, or allowed to present a reasoned case for a period of exemption.

THE NATIONAL CONTEXT FOR ENGAGING, SUPPORTING AND INTERVENING
WITH CHILDREN AND FAMILIES IN CHALLENGING CIRCUMSTANCES

Some ingredients that relate strongly and causally to underachievement at school are beyond the school's capacity or remit to deal with, much as they might try. A greater proportion of children grow up in poverty in the UK than in most other affluent countries, 17% of children by measures applied by UNICEF. UK area child poverty statistics[29] for 2010, which measure child poverty, defined as growing up in families with less than 60% of the national household median income (about £21,500 in 2009/10 before housing costs), indicate that, on average 21.3% of children in England live in poverty. For Thanet, the child poverty level stands at 26.7%, the highest for any area in Kent and the 50th poorest out of the 326 areas of England. Newington has a population of about 4,000. It is divided into three areas for which Super Output Area statistics are collected and published. Two of the three areas are in the bottom 5% in England. This makes those two neighbourhoods 'super poor'.

The UK has a perverse tendency to apply negative labels to whole communities, to vilify them, and to solidify a distinction between the deserving and undeserving poor as if the distinction had a real meaning that can be applied as equally to children in a community as to the adults. The British, arguably most particularly the English, can condemn children born into less favoured family and neighbourhood circumstances by niggardly and poorly judged injections into household budgets (welfare payments) and into local support facilities and services (statutory and voluntary organisations' children and family support projects). Professionals happily use terms like 'Schools Facing Extremely Challenging Circumstances' (SFECC) or 'success against the odds' without seeing that the challenging circumstances or the odds against are socially and politically contrived and sustained conditions. These are issues that central government should act upon, but international comparisons of levels of poverty do not shame UK political parties into radical action as they should. Meanwhile, Ministers for Education are happy to quote OECD's international comparison of educational standards among 15 year-olds in mathematics, science and reading across 65 countries when it suits them. Chapter 10 takes this argument further.

The get-out used by many commentators is an astonishing resort to anecdote and exception, which is a denial or a genuine lack of understanding of notions of likelihoods, probabilities and statistical relationships between variables. Of course, it is always possible to point to poor families whose children prosper and to schools with a poor catchment area where heroic effort raises attainment to near the national norms. However, the *probabilities* remain that schools with children from families with incomes low enough to entitle the children to free school meals will perform at lower levels in terms of attainment – and in terms of attendance, anti-social social behaviour, teenage pregnancies. Most people can understand odds when applied to horse racing and other sporting events and know that odds are associated with past performance in similar conditions. Some horses are just less likely to win and usually run to form. In a more important context, the same reasoning applies to children, families and schools.

CHAPTER 10

It is difficult to be wholeheartedly positive about government programmes to intervene and support families. The Family Intervention Projects[30] piloted until 2010 in LAs around the country and established under Labour were intensive and worked *with* the families in a no blame way. That initiative was replaced by the coalition government's Troubled Families[31] programme, where there is a different emphasis, one which talks of *demanding* that families change their ways, savings to the tax payer and an implied cycle of criminality if nothing is done. It is as though concern can very easily switch from looking at the benefits to the family and especially the developing children to resentment at public costs and fear of the underclass – with all the vocabulary, stereotyping and rejection that goes with it. Support for such families because it is a morally correct to do so and because the inequalities in income and wealth are so clearly unjust are not standard motives of policy makers.

PARENTS AND FAMILIES ARE THE KEY

Children have as their most important and enduring influence their parents, siblings and extended family. The state needs to prevent the condition of family poverty from being the inhibiting force it currently is and to support families so that they are able to collaborate with, and reinforce schools' educational and developmental efforts. Schools have their part to play which is to reach out, to invite in and to ensure that they relate appropriately to parents to engage their support, practical assistance and partnership. For schools in the more challenging circumstances, this requires more personnel, more time, more funds, more effort and more commitment.

MAKING A WORKING CLASS SCHOOL WORK

INTRODUCTION

This book has focused on one secondary school and its neighbourhood and the school's efforts to raise achievement as well as give a full, rounded developmental experience to its students. It is a school/academy in a poor area engaged in a struggle many will recognise. The struggle is emblematic of how we fund the education of poor people. The Marlowe Academy is like 100 plus other secondary schools in England which, by many measures, do well – but not well enough to keep them out of 'notice to improve', 'special measures' or 'national challenge' territory.

THE INJUSTICE OF POOR CHILDREN AND FAMILIES GETTING POOR SCHOOLS

The story of The Conynham School, which became The Ramsgate School and then the Marlowe Academy, chronicles the catastrophic effects of the poorly regulated education market, the punitive 'driving up standards' policy in England and the refusal to address family poverty as the root of underachievement of poor children. If the education system lets you down during your teenage years, the difficulties of retrospectively gaining qualifications and raising your life chances are huge despite further education colleges, Workers' Educational Association and reports like *Learning Through Life.*[32] The Ramsgate School, in an area of considerable measured disadvantage, was in the national press twice, in 1997 and 2003, as the worst school in England. Its slump to this humiliating position and its rise are chronicled in the earlier chapters but the task of improvement is unfinished.

'Working class' is an indistinct and dated notion but sums up the bundle of manual or low level administrative work, few qualifications, low pay or benefits, culture, housing, poverty, insecurity and abilities and aspirations issues which typify a community or neighbourhood. Schools like The Ramsgate and The Marlowe Academy serve such a community. Such schools can be made to work better for poor children and poor communities if policy and practice were to take a broader and more generous view of the levers for change.

Current approaches to poorly performing schools individualise and psychologise success and failure; these are attributed to the character of individuals or schools. But the solutions to underperformance or low attainment are not to be found only, or even mostly, within the school. That is the big mistake, the con, the injustice. Taking an ecological perspective, there are four environments proposed here where causes and solutions are found: the home, the school, the meso environment or local conditions, and the macro environment. The school is the least powerful of these as long as conditions are not modified in the other three. See Figure 11.1.

ACTION TO ADDRESS INJUSTICE AND POOR EDUCATIONAL PROVISION

The four environments are interdependent. The home environment, particularly the degree of poverty, is affected by local employment opportunities (meso environment), levels of child and family support and the extent of redistributive policies (macro environment). Schools are unfairly subject to the culture of targets and the shaming of failure as well as the promotion of solutions entirely within the school when we know the school is a remarkably minor player in affecting achieved attainment levels, compared to home, class and poverty which are overwhelming correlates.

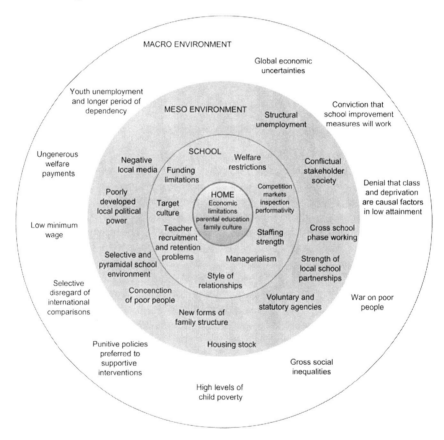

Figure 11.1. Mapping the terrain for social justice and appropriate education for all.

HOME

There are economic limitations stemming from low household income which make life more of a struggle and less predictable. In poorer working class areas, the majority of families are not equipped with backgrounds that enable them to guide children through schooling. They do not grasp what counts as support for homework or reading and, when a child has difficulties with a subject, they can provide only limited help, if any, and cannot afford additional tuition. As a starting point, students entering such secondary schools arrive in Year 7, on average, one year behind in basic skills – arguably a situation *allowed* to develop in the primary years and even earlier because of a lack of resources devoted to preventing this disadvantage increasing. Tables in Chapter 9 show how children from poorer homes regularly perform well below those from better off homes and that the Marlowe consistently accepted children whose attainment on entry to the school was well below the average at age 11.

Parental education and not 'knowing your way around' the system compounded by limited social networks that can advise and offer models of success through education can contribute to low aspirations and expectations. In the UK, services, systems and communities are not good at intervening to diminish the impact of negative forces or energetically insert other role models and make new possibilities real. We invest too timidly in this area.

SCHOOL

After all these years of interventions,[33] policy-makers and the general public, still do not fully recognise how very much more difficult it is for schools serving disadvantaged communities to improve. Policy-makers should be well aware of a body of school improvement research which focusses on poor communities, failing schools and schools facing exceptionally challenging circumstances.[34] There is no argument that improving such schools is difficult and expensive. The reason is poverty, the elephant in the room, the dirty word, the injustice most choose not to speak of.[35]

The loss of a major industrial employer, as in former coalfield or declining areas, and the subsequent loss of employment and reduction in income, bring a set of socio-economic problems: physical and mental health issues, migration of the best qualified young people with the knock on effect on educational achievement. As if that is not enough, challenging pupil behaviour, high levels of staff turnover and a poor physical environment often accompany poverty-related factors. Schools in areas such as these have to work harder than neighbours with better intakes to improve and stay effective, even if judged solely on the basis of government 16+ floor targets. They find it harder to improve, harder to maintain an upward trajectory and their work is vulnerable to being derailed by staff sickness, change of head or teacher turnover, and, as in the case of the Marlowe, the change in the 16+ floor target, the arbitrary moving of goalposts.

Much publicity has been given to those few schools that make dramatically rapid improvements, often under the leadership of those whom the media term 'superheads'. As previous chapters have shown, sustained improvement depends crucially on sustained investment and effort, 'going the extra mile' and 'exceeding normal efforts'.[36] Teachers in schools facing challenging circumstances have to work harder and be more committed than their peers in more favourable socio-economic circumstances – and must maintain the effort to sustain that improvement if success is not to be short-lived and fragile.

Chapter 9 has given the ingredients that make a successful school. Saying that the school *works* means that it provides necessary inputs and stimulation to promote the development and advancement of the children or young people that it serves so that they may function well in the society of which they are part, balancing the advantages that education can bestow upon the individual with the collective good that results from a rounded citizenry and a capable workforce. Whatever the school, and whatever the community or class it serves, *the teaching must be good* and the teacher-student relationships appropriate to excite or enlist the cooperation of the learners. Good teaching involves stimulating material, differentiated work for students, sound monitoring and corrective action when students fall behind or otherwise lose engagement. It requires an appropriate curriculum, one which connects with the aspirations and expectations of the local community in all its variety and does not close off options. Schools in challenging circumstances have *staff recruitment and retention problems* and *staffing strength* cannot always be maintained, which might be due to geographical location or more 'attractive' nearby schools to work in; – both are certainly the case with The Marlowe Academy. The *style of relationships* and management has a big impact on the balancing act necessary to keep and develop staff who can 'make it', while moving on those who will not.

Relationships with the community must be extensive and really reach families. There must be services to compensate for what cannot or is not provided by the family base; this is the extended school, community school or full-service school. Parents are the chief sponsors of students at the school. Where there is an understanding on the parents' part and quite clear reinforcement of the school's culture, work and goals, the way forward is eased. Where this shared understanding and commitment is not automatically there, the school will either need to build it and strive to raise parents' commitment to the school and its work or it must compensate for lack of support and substitute its own influences to act as a bridge and enable the students to progress optimally. To the extent that *funding limitations* can be overcome, it may be possible to carry out a broader range of functions and extend the *restricted welfare role*. Other compromises which the school in challenging circumstances struggles to make acceptable (for government and Ofsted) include the *target culture*, which operates unsympathetically towards them, as does the whole business of *competition*, *market*s and *performativity*. The barriers to success are stacked high against them.

The *style of relationships* between staff and the student community is also important since if students have a sense of belonging and a share in the ownership they will have a basic desire to attend. Attendance is a critically important indicator of a struggling school's improvement; in The Ramsgate School the high absence rate was identified as interrupting continuity in learning and when relationships changed in the Marlowe (see Figure 8.4, Chapter 8), attendance rates rose impressively to close to the national average.

Resources are key to school transformation but funding has to be targeted and monitoring robust to ensure the desired effects and outcomes. School funding formulae are sophisticated. The basic Age Weighted Pupil Unit (AWPU) of funding for schools is based on pupil numbers. There is additional funding which takes account of such factors as: proportion of children with special needs, deprivation indicators, and English as an additional language. Taking the AWPU and all the other additional payments and calculating a new pupil unit funding for schools makes it plain that some schools will receive as much as 50% more per pupil than others. The relevant figures for 2010 in the 10 Thanet LA secondary schools were that the three grammar schools received around £5,000 per student while two of the secondary high schools received over £8,000 per pupil The figure for the non-LA Marlowe Academy, while not directly comparable, would have been over £9,000 per pupil. The differential is not enough. Schools facing extremely challenging circumstances need still more to support their children's development.

Teachers know that there are circumstances where students will learn almost unaided and get good passes at GCSE, while there are other situations where groups need to be small, the number of adults present large, and the skill level of teachers has to be very high. Therefore, funding should reflect these needs to ensure better recruitment and retention of teachers and support initiatives like breakfast clubs, home visiting, youth work, counselling etc for the school should be better equipped to fulfil its role in its community.

MESO ENVIRONMENT

The meso environment is that space between school and national policies and comprises local conditions such as structural unemployment, quality of housing stock, facilities and local discretion about the strength of local school partnerships. In many areas with schools in challenging circumstances there is a concentration of poor people in relatively poor housing with larger families resulting in some overcrowding.

Distinctive in the Thanet case and The Marlowe Academy's *selective and pyramidal school environment* is the already rigged local education market which prevails in LAs like Kent. Thirty-one percent of Thanet 11–16 year olds attend grammar schools. Denominational schools and those in 'nice' neighbourhoods have intakes of pupils from more affluent families. This leaves those schools which serve a block of largely public housing with the biggest educational challenges.

There are claims that where *local school partnerships* develop, and are not overly inhibited by the perceived need to compete, schools which might otherwise struggle have reportedly prospered in networked communities of schools – though it is not clear whether effects endure[37]. Partnership schools might share staff where one school suffers shortages in a particular subject. There may also be agreed changes in the composition of catchment areas or the school intakes within partnerships.

Cross school phase working can also help the collective effort to prevent so many children falling so far behind. Life chances depend on being qualified to proceed to the next level. To achieve the government's floor target at KS 4, it is poor *policy and practice* to begin at 14 or even 11 years of age if the prior learning has not taken place. Graphs and tables in Chapter 8 which show that children are behind at very early stages of their lives, make it plain that a life span approach needs to be adopted. In any neighbourhood, those teaching at secondary school have a stake in making sure that the earlier, even pre-school experience and earliest learning is effective.

Schools and neighbourhoods can suffer from **negative local media**, recently made more powerful by electronic media which anyone can input into and access. Political power is generally not strong in the promotion of the interests of economically disadvantaged areas and **voluntary and statutory agencies** may be overwhelmed and fail to make a difference.

MACRO ENVIRONMENT

The macro environment covers everything beyond the local area including national culture, media, legislation and governmental decisions affecting education policy, the creation of poverty and the increase in inequality, all within **global economic uncertainties** which also impact disproportionately on poor people.

Eliminating, or substantially reducing, the **high levels of child poverty** and reducing gross inequalities are necessary elements in the strategy to reduce the achievement gap. Plain low income and all the stress, worry, poor health and under-appreciation that go with it undermine a family's ability to support their children through education. You cannot make a working class school succeed on the same terms as a school for middle class people. Poverty, poverty, poverty is a grinding and weighty collection of disadvantages and the British know how to create and maintain inequalities of income and wealth better than almost any other European nation; Figure 8.1 shows only Ireland and Portugal are worse in terms of child poverty. Measures of inequality put the UK well behind France, Netherlands, Germany and of course the Scandinavian countries; only Ireland and Latvia were worse on inequality[38]. We delude ourselves, as citizens, social scientists or professional educators, if we do not acknowledge this and act on this knowledge.

The reality is that education in England remains a significant institution for *reconfirming* middle class status and the income and wealth potential that goes with it. Education has served as a corrective to inequalities and as a means of social mobility to a far lesser extent than we are encouraged to believe. The idea of a meritocracy is not borne out by evidence.

Inequality is socially produced and sustained whether in terms of ownership of resources or earned income. **Low minimum wage** levels and **ungenerous welfare payments** are the most obvious political decisions. Again we compare badly with most of our European neighbours and show a **selective disregard of international comparisons** where these show the UK up badly.

What proportion of the country's wealth is it acceptable for the richest 10% of the population to own?[39] In the UK in 2010, the richest 10% of households had 31% of the total income, a big rise since 2000. The poorest 10% had just over 1% of the national income.[40] The Wilkinson and Springett[41] book, referred to in Chapter 1, has as its key message that more equal societies do better at almost everything to do with citizens' well-being. The UK government should be taking note and acting on this information, especially in the light of the following data.

The Barnardo's website (2012) claims:

3.9 million children live in poverty in the UK, that's almost a third of children. Poverty is the single greatest threat to the well-being of children and families. Growing up in poverty can **affect every area of a child's development** – social, educational and personal. One third of British children are forced to go without at least one of the things they need, such as three meals a day or adequate clothing. (original bold print).[42]

If we can recognise the huge impact poverty has on the educational prospects of children, if we can set aside all those exceptions we remember of the working class grammar school child made good, then coherent, multi-level programmes can be developed to enhance the life chances of poorer children. Venomous talk of Chavs, teenage hooligans and feckless parents needs to be challenged as representing attitudes which are terms inaccurately and unjustly used to label large sections of the population. It is an important step towards the fair allocation of resources to those less well off that negative stereotypes are countered and do not contribute to the demonisation and denigration of people less fortunate than the norm. It may be possible to move forward with redistributive policies which will favour poorer neighbourhoods if the negative stereotyping is effectively countered.

The drilling which the Marlowe teacher admitted they had adopted to get good grades in 2011 should not be at the expense of the 'deep learning' to which one of the students referred.

A good, satisfying and successful secondary school experience has to be built on success from early stages. Closing the gap between the attainment of poor and affluent students is not proceeding very quickly in England. In The Marlowe, progress was good up to 2009, but the handicap of the intake at 11 was huge and the Labour administration change in the GCSE floor target to include maths and English was a gigantic disruptive blow, aggravated further by the coalition government's subsequent devaluing of vocational qualifications.

Cross school and cross phase collaborative working could become recommended structural configurations. Geoffrey Canada's work on the Harlem Children's Zone[43] may not offer the best parallels for solutions in Thanet, Kent, UK, but it involves earliest interventions in schools and families following through to college graduation, highly resourced, relentless effort, constant monitoring and extensive coordinated outreach initiatives. Policies and practice that interrupt the adverse force of poverty remain absent in the UK. It is scandalous that there are 'odds against' succeeding and the situation should never be like what the American sociologist, Gans terms, 'war against the poor',[44] yet it almost is.

GUILT AND BLAME

The above sections catalogue mistaken focuses, malign policies, intentional disregard of international comparisons and a shocking capacity to sustain punitive and damaging initiatives, The guilt that some feel, but all should feel, takes its impetus from of three cardinal moral acts or omissions: acceding to the misguided pressure on schools to do a job they are not equipped to do; colluding in the decisions to target attention on school effectiveness and school leadership when it has been shown that the school only accounts for, at best, 20% of the difference in student achievement; and tolerating high levels of child poverty and low levels of social mobility which are worse in the UK than in other comparable countries.

Alma Harris finds it inescapable that, 'the dominant factors affecting school performance in the former coalfield areas are those associated with extreme social disadvantage'[45] and that changes like providing more employment opportunities (ie less poverty), projects like Education Action Zones and changing school intakes (ie, richer kids) make a difference. Harris is amongst researchers in the school effectiveness/school improvement field who have moved to the idea of contextualising improvement initiatives. By 2012, there seems to be a consensus that the extraordinary effort to close the gap in attainment in high poverty areas and in schools facing extremely challenging circumstances, continues to have a sustainability problem and that effective leadership is only part, and maybe a quite vulnerable and minor part, of the solution.

Richard Rothstein writes of the situation in the United States that, 'the gap in average [academic] achievement can probably not be narrowed substantially as long as the United States maintains such vast differences in socioeconomic conditions'.[46]

Martin Thrupp[47] claims similarly that:

Technical solutions will never be enough, schools and teachers in low SES (socio-economic-status) settings may only be held partly responsible for addressing poor achievement and that educational quality in low-SES settings will not be able to be substantially improved without redistributive policies of various kinds.

New Labour and 'third way' did not work sufficiently to reduce child poverty or deliver redistributive policies. New Labour is the 'second party of capital'[48]. Freeing up competition in industry and commerce, making competition drive up standards, enabling failure to be punished, ensured that some losers, with children chief amongst them, must be tolerated for the overall economic good of the majority.

There is an international context to the macro environment in which the UK shows up poorly and as ungenerous to those in deprived circumstances. Indeed, levels of inequality should be recognised as created and sustained by successive government policies and, by extension all of us, the electorate. Great effort has been expended on improving schools, their internal workings, the quality of teaching, the design of the curriculum, the provision of additional services, inputs and opportunities. But this is about the 10 to 20% of difference that can be made on educational attainment. It is the 80 to 90% related to socio-economic status that could make a significant change[49]. It is a continuing deceit by academics, political parties and the media not to recognise this. It is a contrived injustice that raising the attainment levels of students from deprived circumstances and reducing the gap in 5A*-C GCSE grades obtained by richer and poorer students rests on *school* improvement. It is scandalous that elites continue to have unchallenged benefits and advantages and the army of middle class professionals working on anti-poverty initiatives continue to draw decent incomes and academics thrive on producing evaluations and more theoretical writings. And, yes, I am one.

The tiresome dismay at limited success and researchers' high-minded accounts of 'what works' do little to change the statistics of failure year on year and the diminished life chances of children whose misfortune it is to be born into poor families. Why there is not rage at this is the big question. There should be fierce anger that people live out their lives in areas of concentrated deprivation, high crime and poor services. An educated electorate should be persuaded to vote for policies that ensure fairer shares and that extremes of wealth and poverty are reduced. The public acceptance of growing inequalities in income in the UK is quite astonishing.

Ben Levin wrote the following in 2006, which sums up the idea that we may be kidding ourselves that we are making a difference, or even that we really intend to:

> When I read ... papers about improving schools in high poverty communities, I do not get a sufficient sense of anger or outrage. School improvement is really a deeply political activity – not in the partisan sense but in the sense that it is bound up with ideas about improving society and about fair chances for students. Yet, the literature on school improvement is almost studiously apolitical.[50]

Poverty, the scale of inequality and the support for school improvement which focuses on the individual school in this blinkered way are indeed political constructions. In England, political and intellectually deceitful choices are made **not** to associate school failure with poverty and class, which makes the punitive approaches to struggling schools not just crude but dishonestly incompetent. The blame is surely shared across many levels from political parties, which avoid the challenge of tackling injustice and inequality, down to the professionals and citizens who do not vigorously confront the arguments about *excuses* for failure with the data on *reasons* which are associated with extreme levels of child and family poverty and embarrassing levels of inequality.

Talk of 'success against the odds', breaking the cycle of poverty or of 'schools in (extraordinarily) challenging circumstances' simply avoids the empirical question of what forces create these challenging circumstances. The corresponding moral questions are about whether these circumstances should be tolerated, whether the struggle should be so hard and the outcomes almost always so low for an identifiable proportion of the population. Schools like The Marlowe Academy will, decades hence, work better for working class people and the odds will favour them making their rightful, recognised contribution to student advancement if the forces creating poverty are tackled at the macro level. Collectively, the screams must be louder and more diverse in order to promote redistributive economic policy and greater sustained effort to break the link between impoverished family background and future occupation and income.

POSTSCRIPT

THE STORY TO AUGUST 2012

Another year in the life of The Marlowe Academy, a sudden change of leadership and a new style, drive and pressure to address weaknesses which Ofsted inspections and GCSE results threw up. This appended section describes the changes from September 2011 to August 2012, the reasons given for them, the strategies employed by the new management and the results achieved. We must not lose sight of the enduring nature of the challenge facing the Academy and those schools facing similar circumstances and serving similar communities. Targeting the school/academy is missing the point when almost all the forces creating the challenges to educational achievement lie with the levels of poverty and deprivation of the young people and their families.

INSTANT CHANGE

The threat to the Marlowe leadership was obvious through 2010/11 with the Academy GCSE results standing at 14% 5A*-C including maths and English in 2010; this put the Academy in the bottom six secondary schools in the country. Additionally, the Ofsted *notice to improve*, delivered in April 2011, would result at the next inspection in being taken out of that category or put in *special measures*[51]. Then came the disappointment of only 20% 5A*-Cs in 2011. Two missed targets! Mr J's departure was agreed before the end of August; some hardened administrators would say with hindsight they had waited a year too long. Yet the chair of trustees, Mr De Haan, could look back on the Academy's six years and say that Mr J had been successful: he had implemented the plan set down by the trustees for a vocational school that would meet the needs of this community, where many of the young people had felt disenfranchised.

Mr J transformed the school. His agreed mission was to provide a safe place for these children; a school they would respect; a place they would want to come to; to get the GCSE equivalent pass rate up to the national average. He was successful in all this. He started a 6th form to get as many children as possible to tertiary education, 'to have a passport to escape from the community which they had been brought up in'. So much had been positive.

Mr J was pressured, however little he showed it, and he was having to listen to two consultants brought in by the trustees, make changes that he was not entirely in sympathy with and at a speed and harshness that were not his style. The trustees had set up an improvement board which met monthly and was sometimes attended by a representative from the DfE. Mr J's 2009 video recording affirmed that he would not leave and that the Marlowe was 'his baby'. Later, it was as if this was becoming the child he was less keen to rear with tighter monitoring, sterner

143

application of competence arrangements and the sort of toughening of discipline that led to more fixed period exclusions.

Once the 2011 results were in on August 25th at 21% 5A*-Cs, revised down to 20%, there was instant reaction from the DfE and interest from the Schools Commissioner whose principal focus was 'turning around school under-performance and championing the growth of academies'. This amounted to near directives to take action and engage the services of the Academies Enterprise Trust (AET)[52] and the intervention team they could provide. The engagement in the problem from the very top, the speed of change and the calibre of staff assigned to the Marlowe were impressive. This was a school they did not want to see fail.

The departure of Mr J and the arrival of Mr W from the AET took place in under two weeks. Mr W, of the AET, was instructed by his boss on 31st August to accompany him to The Marlowe Academy very early the following morning, met with Mr De Haan and his team in Sandgate, was grilled and then taken alone to the Marlowe to meet with the Senior Leadership Team, who had just learned of Mr J's departure. Further discussions took place with AET about what they would bring and achieve. Mr W was confirmed as interim principal and walked into The Marlowe Academy theatre on 5 September to meet around 200 staff.

THE INTERVENTION

AET had to accelerate the improvement and initially thought they could reach 35% 5A*-Cs including maths and English in the summer 2012. This was revised down to 30% after their appraisal of the issues and problems. The new team was 2.6 staff, a full time principal and vice-principal, and two part-time associate principals (0.6), drawn from a reputedly quality group that had worked well the previous year. Six Advanced Skills Teachers (ASTs) were also promised, but these proved more difficult to get of the calibre and type the principal wanted.

Mr W's team was compared very favourably, in comparison with the consultant input of the year before, in its intensity, focus and determination. Mr De Haan, as the philanthropic sponsor, wanted to give them all they needed and was in discussion with the DfE about intervention support, which it seems they were reluctant to provide. This intensity of intervention does not come cheap. The additional funding required for the year, estimated at over half a million pounds, was the subject of continuing 'discussions' in September 2012. To understand the scale and dimensions of the challenge, AET brought in a consultancy group, INCYTE, to carry out an Ofsted style inspection. They reported that, of the 60+ lessons observed, 54% were inadequate.

Mr W knew the challenges, stating, 'No other school has a profile like this, and no school has a reputation like this' but, had the Marlowe reached 25%, a big jump from the previous year's 14%, AET would not have been called upon. Nevertheless, Mr W did not see the task as only about the headline percentage of 5A*-C grades including maths and English: 'There was a significant and holistic challenge in this academy', and he reeled off the areas found lacking:

- the teaching and learning profile (quality of teaching and learning)
- the curriculum (adjustment away from vocational towards academic)

- deployment of staff especially support staff
- policies and procedures and how they are adhered to
- the business of scrutiny and challenge
- inclusion (bringing down over 1,000 fixed term exclusions)
- the sixth form 'which seemed to be ambling along'
- staffing (absence figures were high)
- behaviour and discipline
- attainment of 5A*-Cs as well as 5A*-G (too many had left with nothing).

From his experience, Mr W said this academy felt like special measures straightaway. He made it clear that he would never have taken on the job without knowledge that his own AET team was behind him. Initial discussions with Mr De Haan indicated that there would be an intervention budget and he knew what he would require–the colleague who had been with him in the previous academy interim headship, the overall Director of Challenge and Intervention in AET, 'the sharpest tool in the box'. She would lead on the strategic intervention in teaching and learning, to develop the core plans, show how to put in milestones and to review their achievement. His experience was that the leadership had to work 24 hours a day and 'it soaks the life out of you in a school like this', if you don't divide the role up. This year had to be 'a monster in terms of impact' and his role was to model and lead, to present a clear vision, valuing and developing people, establishing a positive culture and to be the visible face of authority on the ground and in the corridors. While this was a cohesive core team, it was relatively small[53]. Mr W was from the outset able to remodel the existing leadership team members into *the team* that was to do the job. There was to be no culling of staff. There was much targeted mentoring and coaching to establish an accountable, distributed management system. The five page Development Plan for 2011/12 detailed interventions, milestones and targets. Among these were: the Accelerated Reading initiative with monthly reading age updates; 44 students to be prepared for the English Baccalaureate. Progressive Educational Tools[54] were contracted to make an intense input with 60 Year 11 students and this guaranteed 3+ GCSEs in the space of a week. The total effort from the AET team and the leadership group was massive, progressively adjusted and carefully monitored.

Before all the input had taken effect, the November 2011 inspection, led by HMI, put the school into *special measures* and the inspectors' judgements absolutely mirrored those of the INCYTE team. Mr De Haan reported the judgement as 'heart-breaking for me ... unjust and perverse to disregard the capacity that AET had brought in'. Lengthy arguments with Ofsted followed and, most unusually, the publication of the report was delayed until March 2012. The improvement plan and the 'outstandingly good team' that AET had put in were regarded by the trustees as all they could have done, accomplished with astonishing speed, had been almost a directive from the DfE. Still the report judged almost everything *inadequate* (grade 4): the overall effectiveness of the school; its capacity for sustained improvement, outcomes for individuals and groups; effectiveness of leadership and management in embedding ambition and driving improvement; even its sixth form. It was a shockingly negative report. Being only half a term into AET's involvement with The Marlowe Academy, they could feel relaxed about the judgement – had even expected it – and anticipated that special measures would bring funding with it. Mr De Haan angrily made the point, after the first monitoring visit in March 2012 recording 'satisfactory progress', that any progress had NOTHING to do with being put into *special measures* and NO extra funding had come. The inspection's role had been entirely negative.

The second monitoring visit in early July also judged that progress was satisfactory; they had hoped for 'good'. As Mr De Haan saw it, the school had been forced to move away from its vocational curriculum and other changes were at the expense of the calm and homely place it had been. AET had made it more conventional and some of the 'proud to be different' aspects not seen as paying off were discarded. Even the 8.30 – 5.00 school day ceased in September, 2012.

THE IMPACT

AET had predicted in the summer term 2012 that they would achieve all round improvements as set out below. In August 2012, Mr W said, 'We were spot on with our predictions, except in English[55] where examination boards had changed the grade boundaries!' There was disappointment, even outrage, that the grade boundary changes had been made shortly before the end of the courses and no one in schools knew until days before the results came out. There were reportedly tears from students who had been reliably predicted the higher grades, since so much was already assessed.

Achievement at 16+ at The Marlowe Academy 2010/11 to 2011/12

	2010/11 results	*2011/12 predicted*	*2011/12 results*
5A*-C inc M & E	20	*32*	20
5A*-C	63	*87*	80
5A*-G	76	*93*	93

There was pleasure in the increases in the 5A*-C and the 5A*-G percentages and that the expected number of NEETs was down to 4%, that is seven students and these were non-attenders. Attendance had gone up and exclusions down. Mr W left recording that it had been an honour to be part of The Marlowe Academy and generously attributed the achievements to the staff and students who could feel proud.

THE LESSONS

The Ramsgate School and the Marlowe Academy remain a place where it is a struggle to provide the standard of education and achieve the outcomes the local area deserves for its children. National poverty policies do little to address that severe underlying set of forces that make schooling difficult to benefit from. National education policies, adjustments to success criteria and shaming bottom tier schools[56] to achieve all exacerbate the problem. The Academy has to work very hard to recruit and retain quality staff. During the school day, all staff, including the most senior, need to be focussed, available, supervising and interacting to ensure the best can be achieved. It is unbelievably wearing and staff need to feel a pride in what is achieved.

The presence of *a team* was shown again to be vital. Mr H had it, Mr J marshalled a larger group and Mr W began his year as a team of 2.4 but backed by a strong governing body/trustees and brought on board existing staff. If the team crumbles the Academy could regress to the 'dreadful' state it was in the early 2000s.

The enforced compromises with the national requirements are not all sensible. Mr H had been utterly single-minded; Mr J had a subtle, finely balanced, progressively implemented dream; Mr W saw the need for holistic development if the critical, required level of results were to be achieved in under a year.

THE PROSPECTS

A new principal began in September 2012 to continue the job. The Marlowe Academy is an iconic school from which many lessons can be learned. The upward trajectory can be driven forward and results and reputation can be improved. Still one should not leave in the background the massive disadvantages of poverty inflicted on the young such that they are, on average, measurably behind from the earliest assessments.

METHODOLOGY

BEING A RESEARCHER OR JUST NOSING AROUND

As a researcher with 35 years experience, I knew about the steps to take, the ethical considerations, mainly about confidentiality, and what count as good approaches to interviews as well as how to make notes in less structured situations. This study was different from those for which I have been funded and was a personal journey without an imposed agenda or timescale. The study, carried out over two year period (September 2009 – August 2011), involved the following:

– gathering documentary historical material on the school and the neighbourhood
– organising local, national and international data of relevance
– being present in the school and recording what was happening, relationships and interactions, inside classrooms and outside. My great pleasure was sitting in the atrium area of the Academy with school life going on around me;
– interviews with current school staff and pupils, staff and pupils from earlier times and education officers and advisers
– Interviews with family members, residents on the Newington estate, some of whom were parents of pupils who had children currently or previously at the Conyngham, Ramsgate or Marlowe school and with professionals who worked on the estate
– Walking around, chatting with people, snooping perhaps.

While I operated with a certain informality, I nonetheless asked permission for access to workers from line managers and for entry to any meetings or workplaces; I was never where I was not expected. Anyone I spoke to and noted information I might use was told what I was doing and assured that no person would be recognisable from anything I wrote. If they were recognisable, I would return to see that the text was OK by them.

The research was submitted to the University of Greenwich Research Ethics Committee and there was rigorous adherence to confidentiality agreements and sensitivity to the ongoing work in the school and to very personal information given by families. Some of the descriptions have been changed so that individuals would not be identifiable.

Gathering Documentary and Historical Material

This involved minutes of governors' meeting from the KCC Archives for the period 1981–1999, local newspaper archives at the Margate and Ramsgate public library, Ofsted inspection reports going back to 1997 and office files from KCC staff relating to the 2000–2005 period. There were also web searches on such diverse topics as the Conyngham family, national press reporting on the school and the Conyngham Reunion network

Organising Local, National and International Data of Relevance

The school, the Newington area, and the social class and economic challenges faced here, were to be seen against a wider background. This is not a story about free will and individual responsibility operating where all have equal life chances. Data comparing countries' welfare generosity, national data demonstrating severe inequalities and local data showing multiple deprivations are important as the limiting factors of life here.

Present in the School, Recording Events, Relationships and Interactions, Inside Classrooms and Outside

I shadowed classes on three days. This was spread over the period and over age and ability groups. More often I sat in the vast, high ceiling open area, kidding myself I was a writer in residence and I drafted material on my laptop, spoke with staff or pupils who sat at my table and observed 'goings-on' as the school day progressed. From this I sought a sense of life in the school and contacts with others who could answer my questions as they arose. I was in the school for the equivalent of 20 days, not enough to get to the bottom of how a community functions in all its different facets – but what is enough?

Interviews with School Staff, Current Pupils, Staff and Pupils from Earlier Times and Education Officers and Advisers

In all, 24 staff were interviewed including all the headteachers of the Conyngham and Ramsgate Schools and the Marlowe except the first headteacher, who had died. Some were interviewed more than once and many interviews were digitally recorded. Three education officers, including the Director of Education were recorded and 20 pupils were interviewed, mostly singly but two were group interviews. Additionally there were lots of incidental conversations over lunch or while sitting in the open area which probably belong in the 'just being present in the school' description above.

Interviews with Residents on the Newington Estate, Parents of Current or Past Pupils and with Professionals who Worked on the Estate

I interviewed five families who had different experiences of life generally and of the schooling available to their children. Most of these interviews happened in their homes and often several other family members were present, but in only one case was an adult male family member a contributor. Twelve past pupils were interviewed covering the whole period of the school's existence; some of these were from the families who were so hospitable and wonderfully open in telling their stories.

Walking Around, Chatting, 'Snooping'

The estate is an area which does not parade its deprivation – and some would reject that word. The shop keepers offered opinions, ordinary people, once over their suspicion, gave their views on the area and just walking around which I did on six occasions, once in the late evening, during the period gave a feeling of the safety and community ethos.

NOTES

CHAPTER 2

[1] The Conyngham (pronounced Cunningham) family owned large tracts of land between Canterbury and the Thanet coast, including coalfields and the land upon which the estates and the school were built. The family 'seat' is Castle Slane, County Meath, Ireland. Henry Conyngham was a courtier and politician of the regency era and had the titles of Viscount Slane, Earl Mount Charles and Marquis of Conyngham (yes, that is just one person) and later Lord Minster of Minster Abbey Kent. Much of this advancement happened after his marriage in 1794 to Elizabeth, who quickly became a favourite mistress of the Prince Regent. When he became King George IV in 1820, she was established as his main mistress and remained so through to his death in 1830.

When Elizabeth departed from court at the death of the king, there were conflicting reports of whether she left for Canterbury with 'wagonloads of plunder' or selflessly refused all the plate and jewels the king had bequeathed her. Henry Conyngham died in 1832, but Elizabeth reached the age of 92. She died in 1861at Patrixbourne near Canterbury in Kent having outlived all but one of her five children. A large wall plaque to the memory of Elizabeth, first Marchioness Conyngham is in St Mary's church, Patrixbourne, in pride of place to the left of the altar, and other windows and large tombstones to later marquises and marchionesses testify to the family's status. The information board in the churchyard remarks coyly that Marquis Henry 'and particularly his wife, a great beauty, were friends of George IV'.

[2] Gill Evans's (2006) *Educational Failure and Working Class White Children in Britain*, (Basingstoke: Palgrave) describes, as sociologists from decades back have described, how distant formal education is from the lives of working class families and the barriers to their engagement with it. The educational historian, Gary McCulloch, in *Failing the Ordinary Child? The theory and practice of working-class education* (1998, Buckingham: Open University Press) records how class based education has persisted unscathed through all sorts of changes. He writes that ordinary children 'have indeed been failed, not so much by neglect as by the contradictions of class based provision and the illusions to which it gave rise'. He calmly expresses the view that we should expect new ways to be devised to fail the ordinary child as time goes on. In the 14 years since his book appeared, and with more than a decade of a labour government, this has proved to be true.

[3] The Runnymede Trust report (2009) *Who cares about the white working class*, (London: Runnymede). The Sutton Trust and the Joseph Rowntree Foundation have also led the way in raising the issues and exploring options in relation to educational and other inequalities.

[4] Richard Wilkinson and Kate Pickett published, in 2009, *The Spirit Level: Why More Equal Societies Almost Always Do Better*. (London: Allen Lane). It was widely acclaimed. It did, however, lead to unusually aggressive responses. Notable amongst them were Christopher Snowden's *The spirit level delusion* (Monday Books). The Institute of Economic Affairs journalist, Niemietz (www.iea.org.uk/blog/a-superb-critique-of "the-spirit-level"), heralded this book as 'a laugh', and, along with other right-leaning writers and publications, attacked the data, the analysis and even the authors. Snowden maintains a website for a continuing, negative selection of critiques: spiritleveldelusion.blogspot.co.uk/

[5] The bar graph showing infant mortality in Sweden by social class shows equal sized columns. There is practically no difference between social class I and V. In England and Wales, the bars show ever rising numbers of deaths as you go down the social class gradient. The paper is dated, but there is little reason to suppose the comparison does not still hold. See Leon, D. A., Vågerö, D. and Olausson, P. O. (1992) 'Social class differences in infant mortality in Sweden: comparison with England and Wales' in, *British Medical Journal* 305(6855): pp. 687–691.

[6] Herbert Gans, a Black American sociologist wrote in 1995 a provocative book entitled, *The War against the Poor: The Underclass and Antipoverty Policy* (New York: Basic Books). Two central

theses I can recall are: there are elaborate ways for labelling the poor which marginalise them, question their worth, locate blame in them and justify minimal intervention with them; the poor benefit the better off sections of the population financially – providing jobs dealing with them – and emotionally – making us feel good that we give professional support or a little to charity to help them out.

[7] The coalition government's strategy on 'troubled families' uses language more aggressively and negatively than was used in the labour government's Family Intervention Project.

CHAPTER 4

[8] Partridge's 1966 book, *The Secondary Modern School*, states that, 'Perhaps the success of certain schools has only been bought at a cost of failure to many others. If the introduction of a Comprehensive system compels all our administrators and teachers to face the problems of educating all our children, and especially those 25% of present day Secondary Modern children who leave without achieving a satisfactory level of literacy, then the consequent upheaval will have been more than justified'. Kent did not go down that route. For many of the LAs, the problem of the bottom 25% remains.

CHAPTER 5

[9] The term *Schools Facing Exceptionally Challenging Circumstances* (SFECC) appeared in 2006 publications. Before that it was Schools in Challenging Circumstances or schools in high poverty areas or in poor neighbourhoods. Examples are below.

Harris, A. & Chapman, C., 2002, *Effective leadership in schools facing challenging circumstances.* Nottingham: National College for School Leadership.

Harris, A. et al, 2006, *Improving Schools in Exceptionally Challenging Circumstances.* London: Continuum.

MacBeath, J. et al, 2007, *Schools on the Edge: Responding to Challenging Circumstances*, London, Paul Chapman.

One can ask if the new term merely obscures the simple 'poverty' driver behind difficulties.

[10] The data indicate that The Ramsgate School had greater proportions of deprived children and more special needs pupils than any other Thanet secondary school.

[11] Inspection report language is and often has been unconstructive in its content but it did sharpen, achieve a degree of focus and was obviously greatly aided by the detailed computerised records offered by Raiseonline. The 1997 report had key issues such as: 'Evaluate progress made and agree short and medium term priorities; Ensure the needs of the most academically able are met'. Later reports and their proposals are less woolly and often more quantitatively measurable. They are still warning shots and then destructive judgements instead of supportive and motivational.

CHAPTER 6

[12] The Ramsgate School was not a Summerhill, Risinghill, not even a Hackney Downs, with conviction teachers united on some liberation journey with working class children. The school was not in London or another large city but in a far-out, neglected corner of England. The schools in the modern era (1995 onwards) which 'fail' are dotted around the country and their uniting characteristic is the poverty of the families from which they draw their intake.

[13] Academic writing and research emphasise professional development and team building, target setting and good teaching. The speed and aggressiveness of The Ramsgate School team's approach was justified by the sense that the failures had gone on too long, nothing else had worked, the children deserved better and no delay was to be tolerated.

CHAPTER 7

[14] TUPE stands for Transfer of Undertakings (Protection of Employment). These are regulations usually called upon when people move to similar employment in an organisation which changes its governance. A school becoming an Academy is the replacement institution and new employer, now no longer operating under local authority regulations, procedures and pension arrangements.

[15] Names of historical figures associated with the area were considered for the Academy's name: Pugin and Moses Montefiore, and the more contemporary Oscar nominee, Brenda Blethyn.

[16] Google it and one explanation is, 'a light, wooden, "green" engineering solution to produce big spans'.

[17] Ed Balls, the Labour government's Secretary of State for Education announced the new target GCSE floor targets for schools as 30% of pupils gaining 5A*-C grades including maths and English in June 2010. Setting new, higher targets appears to be what all UK political parties in power do, regardless of damaging consequences and the Contextual Value Added scores of schools. Some schools have very high CVAs but low proportions meeting the target! These too are punished.

CHAPTER 8

[18] The very high proportion of SEN pupils attracted additional funding. For students with severe and complex needs requiring 25 hours of support, mostly one-to-one, funding had to be applied for. At £8,000 to £12,000 per student, the Academy received in 2010/11 approximately £140,000 extra for ESEN pupils, who should possibly have been in special school.

[19] National Challenge identified secondary schools achieving below the government's floor targets for student achievement. Out of 3,000 schools, the numbers in 2005/06 were 631 (25% of secondary schools). This number fell over the next few years and in 2009/10 it rose to 27 when maths and English were required within the 5 good GCSE passes. In 2010/11, the number not achieving 35% 5A*-C grades (incl maths and Eng) was 129. The Marlowe Academy was sixth from bottom with its 20%.

CHAPTER 9

[20] Figures from the Independent Schools Council, 2011.

[21] The Gini coefficient comparisons can be found at OECD (2011) *Society at a Glance 2011 – OECD Social Indicators* (www.oecd.org/els/social/indicators/SAG)

[22] Refer to Rowntree figures, the Innocenti Report card, Child Poverty Act and the closing the gap.

[23] This reliable finding is from Leon Feinstein's 2003 research, 'Inequality in the early cognitive development of children in the 1970 cohort, *Economica*, Vol 70, no 277.

[24] The political exhortation to 'drive up standards' comes across as peculiarly crude, uninformed and insulting to a profession. It is the language of threat and punishment, about people not doing their job properly or at least to the best of their ability. Again, the academic literature is softer and in search of processes to help a school work better and achieve better.

CHAPTER 10

[25] In 2011, there were nearly 3,000 looked after children in Kent, over half of whom were from outside the county. A disproportionate number were accommodated in Thanet. Thanet secondary schools complained at the additional burdens this placed on them. The Marlowe Academy had as many as 25 at some times.

[26] Joy Dryfoos, in her important 1994 book, *Full-Service Schools. A revolution in health and social services for children, youth and families*, (San Francisco: Jossey-Bass), writing of the American context says, 'Advocates for full-service community schools believe that today's schools cannot possibly take on all the problems of today's children and their parents. The pressures [ ] are enormous, draining teachers' energy and demoralizing administrators, who recognize that there is

more to education than testing. Schools need other agencies to share some of the responsibility. They need help being open all the time, including before and after school, evenings, weekends, and summers. They want access to comprehensive support services, including primary-care health clinics, dentistry, mental health counseling and treatment, family social work, parent education, enhanced learning opportunities, community development, and whatever else is needed in that school community'.

[27] The HighScope Perry Preschool project worked with 123 poor African American families in Ypsilanti, Michigan, USA in the 1960s. It is *the* classic study which showed long-term beneficial effects following one or two years of high quality pre-school experience. The study has not been replicated, the sample was small and hardly representative (except of poor urban Black people, recently moved north from the rural south). It has arguably been misused as giving hope that such limited input at an early stage in the life course will have lasting effects *anywhere*.

[28] Work by psychologists researching brain functions have found significantly less development of frontal lobe activity at 6 months in babies from poorer backgrounds than in those from better off families. Annette Karmiloff-Smith reports such findings in her presentations (2012).

[29] Local Child Poverty Statistics: www.jrf.org.uk/work/workarea/child-poverty. All political parties signed up to the goal of ending child poverty by 2020 and to the Child Poverty Act of 2010 which enshrined this in law. In 2009, 2.6 million children were living in poverty in the UK. This was 800,000 children fewer than were in poverty in 1998. To reach the government target of halving child poverty by 2010, 900,000 more children would have needed to move out of poverty by that year. The UK government's poverty line is where household income is below 60 per cent of the median UK household income. See also The Department for Work and Pensions publication, Households Below Average Income: An analysis of the income distribution 1994/95–2009/10 (May 2011). Internet: research.dwp.gov.uk/asd/hbai/hbai2010/pdf_files/full_hbai11.pdf

[30] Family intervention Projects (FIPS) were originally funded by the Home Office, with the aim of combating crime and anti-social behaviour. This broadened with the involvement of the DCSF. Typically, a project would have a number of workers with social work, health visiting or other social support backgrounds. Each FIP worker would have a caseload of six families at any one time and address issues concerning school attendance, housing, debt, domestic violence, crime and anti-social behaviour, drink and drugs and more serious concerns of child abuse or neglect. The intervention would cost around £7,000, mostly the cost of the worker's time. The calculations were that, on average, an intervention could save £80.000 over following decades. Funding for the initiative ceased to be 'ring-fenced' in 2010 and was superseded by the Troubled Families programme.

[31] The government's Troubled Families Unit has been set up in the Department of Communities and Local Government. The DfE also has a section for 'Families with Multiple Problems'. They define a troubled family is one that has serious problems – including parents not working, mental health problems, and children not in school – and causes serious problems, such as crime and anti-social behaviour, which costs local services a lot of time and money to routinely respond to these problems. The government estimates that there are 120,000 such families costing £9 billion (averaging £75,000 per family per year) though only £1 billion is spent trying to turn around their lives in a targeted, positive way.

The payment-by-results programme will incentivise local authorities and other partners to take action to turn around the lives of troubled families in their area by 2015. The programme pays up to 40 per cent of the LA's costs when success in turning around a family can be shown. Turning troubled families around is said to mean: 'getting children back in the classroom and not wandering the streets committing crime or anti-social behaviour, getting parents onto a work programme and stopping them being such high cost to the taxpayer'.

A quote from the website: 'It is unacceptable to leave the children in these families to lead the same disruptive and harmful lives as their parents. ... We owe it to these families and to their local communities not to excuse their behaviour but to demand that they change their ways'.

www.communities.gov.uk/communities/troubledfamilies/

CHAPTER 11

[32] Tom Schuller and David Watson published *Learning Through Life: Inquiry into the Future for Lifelong Learning (IFLL)* in 2009 (Leicester: The National Institute of Adult Continuing Education (NIACE)). Its messages were fairly radical in the diversion of funding to enrich and simplify opportunities for older learners. There are few signs that the messages have been acted on.

[33] The link between poverty and educational attainment has long been known and amongst the earliest intervention initiatives were the Education Priority Areas (EPAs) of the 1960s. Social mobility has been studied for longer still and concerns about inter-generational worklessness link with both of these themes. The government's recent Child Poverty Innovation pilots (www.education.gov.uk/publications/eOrderingDownload/DFE-RR152.pdf) and the Strategy for Social Mobility (www.dpm.cabinetoffice.gov.uk/sites/default/files_dpm/resources/opening-doors-breaking-barriers.pdf) show this concern continues.

[34] Some of the key authors are: Mel Ainscow, Christopher Chapman, Peter Fleming, Alan Flintham, Alma Harris, David Hopkins, John McBeath, David Reynolds, Hazel Taylor, Mel West, Graham Wright. There is the journal, School Effectiveness and School Improvement: which bills itself as 'an International Journal of Research, Policy and Practice.' Volume 17, Issue 4, December 2006 was largely devoted to improving schools in challenging circumstances. All this is UK based. Activity over 20 years has been considerable and the International Congress for School Effectiveness and Improvement (ICSEI) is the uniting global occasion, meeting at different points in the world in the early part of every year. Can all this activity from top scholars really be missing the point? It's poverty, stupid!

[35] *Schooling the Estate Kids*, like Paul Corrigan's *Schooling the Smash Street Kids* (1979, Macmillan) and Pat Thomson's *Schooling the Rust Belt Kids* (2002, Trentham Books) and many other sociological writings strive to make a convincing intellectual link between entrenched poverty and attainment and limited social mobility. Mortimore and Blackstone's *Disadvantage and Education* (Heinemann, 1982) is an interesting dated text. Other texts worth looking at are: Theodore Cox (Ed.) (2000) *Combating Educational Disadvantage: Meeting the needs of vulnerable children*, London: Falmer Press for an overview in which Peter Mortimore and Geoff Whitty's chapter 10, 'Can schools overcome the effects of disadvantage?', is the most relevant contribution. Ruth Lupton (2005) Social Justice and School Improvement: Improving the quality of schooling in the poorest neighbourhoods, *British Educational Research Journal*, 31.5, reports a study of four struggling schools one of which was The Ramsgate School (unnamed but recognisable to those with local knowledge); she concludes that: high poverty contexts exert downward pressures on quality, and that consistently high levels of quality in schools in the poorest neighbourhoods need to be assured by policy measures that alter their context or, through greater funding, improve their organisational capacity to respond.

[36] This comes from Alma Harris who has probably written most on improving challenging schools. She and colleagues have concentrated on the in-school factors but have written things like the need to 'erode the social and economic barriers to under-achievement,' 'Levels of disadvantage still account, in part, for poor attainment and this relationship is stubbornly resistant to policy intervention,' and, 'patterns of socio-economic disadvantage have to be recognised and, where possible, addressed'. These are asides from the main thrust and may be moving to a rebalancing of thinking and policy proposals.

[37] Mel Ainscow and colleagues (2012, *Developing Equitable Education Systems*, London Routledge) makes this claim: 'School-to-school partnerships are the most powerful means of fostering improvements' (p. 156). They go on to say that an additional ingredient is the engagement with data (as with Ofsted inspections) so that schools can challenge each other and not become too cosy. It could be suggested that this is 'hope over experience' 'cheap if it worked' but even one of their project schools closed!

[38] The UK is more unequal than most other continental countries as illustrated in figure B below. The Gini coefficient gives a number between 0 and 100 where 0 is perfect equality. For the UK in 2010 it was 36. The Gini coefficient measure of income inequality in the UK was higher in 2008/9 than at any time in the previous 30 years.

Figure B: Gini coefficient measure of inequality for affluent countries

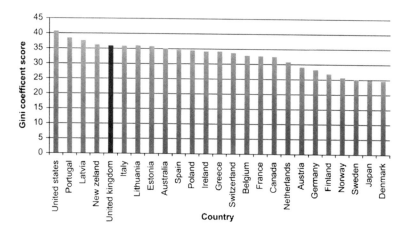

www.nationmaster.com/graph/eco_inc_equ_un_gin_ind-income-equality-un-gini-index

[39] *An Anatomy of Economic Inequality in the UK* (2010) by the National Equality Panel, led by Prof John Hill of the London School of Economics shows the top 10% earning, on average, over 100 times as much as the poorest 10%, a huge increase on 10 years earlier.

[40] Department of Work and Pensions, Aug 2010.

[41] Wilkinson and Springett's diverse list of areas where wellbeing is better where inequality is low is persuasive. In more equal societies, child well-being measures are higher, mental illness rates lower, use of illegal drugs is lower, the teenage birth rate is lower and women's status is higher – to list but a few of the areas.

[42] www.barnardos.org.uk/what_we_do/our_projects/child_poverty/child_poverty_case_studies_stories/child_poverty_claire.htm

[43] Paul Tough's 2008 book, *Whatever it takes*, (2008, New York: Houghton Mifflin Company) is inspirational. It is focussed on the work of Geoffrey Canada and the Harlem Children's Zone where support is given from pre-school through to college.

[44] Herbert Gans wrote a telling account of supposedly anti-poverty policies and produced a list of 'why we need the poor'.

[45] Alma Harris and colleagues (*Raising Attainment in Former Coalfield Areas*, London, DfE , 2003) state that, 'The dominant factors affecting school performance in the former coalfield areas are those associated with extreme social disadvantage' (p. 1). Elsewhere she and colleagues have recognised that 'improvement programmes and initiatives have simply failed to grapple with the broader contextual issues' and have still described schools which 'buck the trend' while warning, 'So we should not be overly optimisitic'. Something of a balancing act.

[46] Rothstein, R. (2004) *Class and Schools*, Washington: Economic Policy Institute (and Teachers College, Columbia University, NY) p. 129.

[47] Thrupp, M. (1999) *Schools Making a Difference: Let's be Realistic! School Mix, School Effectiveness and the Social Limits of Reform*. Buckingham: Open University Press, p. 183.

[48] Stuart Hall's phrase and indicated how far to the right Labour moved to appeal to a wider section of the electorate.

[49] There are various estimates from large data sets about the proportion of attainment that can be attributed to 'the school effect'. Harvey Goldstein, a noted statistician, has said on radio that the proportion is about 10% (*Do Schools Make a Difference*, Radio 4 05.02.12 – www.bbc.co.uk/programmes/b01b9hjs). It is more complicated than that insofar as our datasets are always incomplete. Drawing on the work of Peter Mortimore, Stephen Gorard writes:

'the clear majority of variation in examination outcomes between pupils cannot be explained even by the best data and the most complex of school effectiveness analyses. **Of the 30 to 40% that can be explained, the vast majority of this (75 to 90% of it) is attributable to the prior and individual characteristics of the pupils**' (my emphasis), (Gorard, S. 2010, Education can compensate for society – a bit, in *British Journal of Educational Studies*, 58 (1) – p. 54).

Stephen Ball entitles his paper, 'New class inequalities: Why education policy may be looking in the wrong place! Education policy, civil society and social class' (*International Journal of Sociology and Social Policy* 2010, vol 30.3/4) because, 'a whole variety of studies in the "school effectiveness" field show that on average schools account for somewhere between 5 and 18 per cent of achievement differences between students, after control for initial differences'. Nonetheless, Mel Ainscow and colleagues in their *Developing Equitable Education Systems* (2010, Routledge) mention that equitable developments in education will ultimately depend on government pro-equity policy frameworks, yet they still adhere to the view that, 'In the meantime, it is also the case that **much can be achieved by school change**' (my emphasis) (p. 2). It all depends on what we mean by 'much'!

[50] Levin, B. (2006) Schools in challenging circumstances: A reflection on what we know and what we need to know, *School Effectiveness and School Improvement*, 17.4: 399–407. p. 406.

POSTSCRIPT

[51] A school given a *notice to improve* cannot remain in that category when reinspected and must either show improvement and be judged *satisfactory* or better or be put into *special measures*.

[52] The Academies Enterprise Trust was established in 2008 and has been referred to as the DfE's 'provider of choice' at that time. The organisation runs over 70 academies and has a reputation for swift response and successful action in schools in special measures.

[53] The distinctive features of a team that works to improve a school in challenging circumstances, as shown in the Ramsgate/Marlowe experience are: absolute agreement on the values, targets and methods; huge inputs of time, commitment and effort; speed in first identifying, then addressing, shortcomings; critical size of the team. Arguably the tiny AET team was immediately enlarged by members of the existing SLT whose roles were reassessed and whose members were inducted into and coached on the agreed action plan. AET clearly had s to build on and work with.

[54] Progressive Educational Tools (PET) are an organisation that can be contracted in to make intensive inputs of one to two weeks duration to raise motivational levels, work on skills and (really, don't ask me how) guarantee three and a half GCSEs. 63 students were involved across the whole range of behaviour and commitments but all were on the C/D borderline had the possibility of achieving 5A*-Cs. Only two dropped out. Students were proud of their achievements and certificates they received at the end of the week, their attendance levels rose and remained high in almost all cases.

[55] The English grade boundaries were changed by Ofqual and the three examination boards to ensure there was not 'grade inflation', though the Secretary of State for Education denied any direct pressure. The situation was particularly acute because those who had sat this particular assessment unit in January had had other, more generous, grade boundaries applied and ones to which schools were working. The teacher unions, the Specialist Schools and Academies Trust, LAs and other organisations protested, considered legal action and huge numbers of individual schools appealed students' results. The floor target for schools in 2012 was 40% of students gaining 5A*-C including maths and English. Many schools would be tipped into the National Challenge category by the raised floor target and more still by this reduction in numbers getting an A* – C grade in English.

[56] 'Bottom tier' is Charles Payne's term. In his *So much reform, so little change: the persistence of failure in urban schools* (Cambridge MA: Harvard Education Press, 2008), he laments that 'most discussion of educational policy and practice is dangerously disconnected from the daily realities of urban schools, especially the bottom tier schools' (P5) and that, despite decades of school reform aimed at these institutions, little changes.

INDEX

CPSIA information can be obtained at www.ICGtesting.com
Printed in the USA
BVOW011233290113

311869BV00002B/49/P